OECD Multi-level Governance Studies

Subnational Public-Private Partnerships

MEETING INFRASTRUCTURE CHALLENGES

OECD

BETTER POLICIES FOR BETTER LIVES

This work is published under the responsibility of the Secretary-General of the OECD. The opinions expressed and arguments employed herein do not necessarily reflect the official views of OECD member countries.

This document, as well as any data and any map included herein, are without prejudice to the status of or sovereignty over any territory, to the delimitation of international frontiers and boundaries and to the name of any territory, city or area.

Please cite this publication as:
OECD (2018), *Subnational Public-Private Partnerships: Meeting Infrastructure Challenges*, OECD Multi-level Governance Studies, OECD Publishing, Paris.
https://doi.org/10.1787/9789264304864-en

ISBN 978-92-64-30485-7 (print)
ISBN 978-92-64-30486-4 (pdf)

Series: OECD Multi-level Governance Studies
ISSN 2414-6781 (print)
ISSN 2414-679X (online)

The statistical data for Israel are supplied by and under the responsibility of the relevant Israeli authorities. The use of such data by the OECD is without prejudice to the status of the Golan Heights, East Jerusalem and Israeli settlements in the West Bank under the terms of international law.

Photo credits: © Jeffrey Fisher

Corrigenda to OECD publications may be found on line at: *www.oecd.org/publishing/corrigenda*.

Foreword

Worldwide, infrastructure needs to sustain growth are substantial – estimated by the OECD to be USD 6.3 trillion per year between 2016 and 2030 in energy, transport, water and telecommunications infrastructure. Subnational governments – cities and regions – play a vital role in providing and maintaining infrastructure. They are in charge of almost 60% of public investment on average in OECD countries.

In a tight fiscal environment, it is critical to diversify sources of financing for infrastructure investment and to use public investment to leverage private funding in an effective way. Public-private partnerships (PPPs) represent an alternative to traditional government procurement with the potential to improve value for money. However, PPPs are complex and sometimes risky arrangements that require capacity to undertake them that is not always readily available in governments, in particular at the subnational level. There have been many examples in recent years of PPP failures or misuse, which call for caution in their use.

This report offers guidance on how to improve the governance and implementation of PPPs for infrastructure at the subnational level. The first chapter offers a framework for considering PPPs in a multi-level governance context. It brings together not only ideas and concepts from existing literature, but examples from the three case studies that constitute the remaining chapters: PPPs for local infrastructure in two French cities: Caen and Paris; the United Kingdom's Private Finance Initiative (PFI) projects at the local level; and transportation PPPs in the Commonwealth of Virginia (a US state).

This report supports the implementation of the 2014 *OECD Recommendation of the Council on Effective Public Investment across Levels of Government*. The Recommendation offers good practice guidance through 12 recommendations to address systemic multi-level governance challenges for public investment. Principle 6 ("Mobilise private actors and financing institutions to diversify sources of funding and strengthen capacities") acknowledges the potential benefits that private sector participation can bring to meeting public investment goals.

The report is part of the series *OECD Multi-Level Governance Studies*. It was conducted by the OECD Centre for Entrepreneurship, SMEs, Regions and Cities (CFE). It was developed in cooperation between the Regional Development Policy Committee (RDPC) in CFE that approved the report by written procedure on 30 March 2018 [CFE/RDPC(2018)2] and the OECD Senior Budget Officials Network of Senior PPP and Infrastructure Officials that discussed the report on 27 March 2018.

Acknowledgements

This report was produced by the OECD Centre for Entrepreneurship, SMEs, Regions and Cities (CFE) led by Lamia Kamal-Chaoui, Director. It is part of the multi-level governance Programme of Work of the OECD's Regional Development Policy Committee.

The report is the outcome of a project initiated by the Korean Institute of Public Finance (KIPF). The OECD is grateful to Dr. Junghun Kim, Chair of the OECD Network on Fiscal Relations across Levels of Government and former Vice President of KIPF, for his continuous support to this project.

The report was co-ordinated and supervised by Dorothée Allain-Dupré, Head of Unit, Decentralisation, Public Investment and Subnational Finance. This unit is in the Economic Analysis, Statistics and Multi-level Governance Section, led by Rudiger Ahrend, in CFE.

The report was drafted with contributions from: Dorothée Allain-Dupré; Lee Mizell, Consultant (Chapters 1 and 3); Stephane Saussier, Professor of Economics, Sorbonne Business School, Director of the Economics of PPP research group (Chapter 2); and Jonathan Gifford, Professor at George Mason University and Director of the Center for Transportation Public-Private Partnership Policy with Morghan Transue, editor, George Mason University (Chapter 4). Comments on the draft chapters were received from Rudiger Ahrend, Claire Charbit, Isabelle Chatry, Ian Hawkesworth, Karen Maguire, Varinia Michalun, Ana Maria Ruiz, Camila Vammalle and Isidora Zapata from the OECD Secretariat. Thanks are also extended to Gilbert Probst and Lea Stadtler of the Geneva Public-Private Partnerships Centre for early input for Chapter 1.

The authors gratefully acknowledge the comments and inputs received from the Delegates of the OECD Regional Development Policy Committee and from the Senior Budget Officials Network of Senior PPP and Infrastructure Officials in March 2018.

Sincere thanks are due to the following persons or institutions who contributed to the different case studies:

- France: The author would like to thank: Grégory Berkovicz, from the City Council of Caen; Christian Pierret, former State Minister and former Mayor of Saint-Dié-des-Vosges; and Damien Botteghi, Head of the Legal Affairs Directorate in the City of Paris. Comments received from Salim Bensmail, Director of the *Mission d'appui au financement des infrastructure* are also warmly acknowledged.
- United Kingdom: Sincere thanks are extended to Andrew Bruce of Scottish Futures Trust, Alastair Watson of Local Partnerships, Professor David Heald of the University of Glasgow, and Hera Miah of the Public Private Partnerships Team, Infrastructure and Projects Authority, for their valuable insights and contributions to this case study.

- United States: The authors gratefully acknowledge assistance in fact-checking and reviewing the document from the Virginia Office of Public-Private Partnerships.

Thanks are also due to Julie Harris for editing and formatting the manuscript and to Cicely Dupont-Nivore who prepared the final publication.

Table of contents

Tables

Figures

Boxes

Executive summary

Most public private partnerships (PPPs) occur at the subnational level

The world needs more and better infrastructure. Demand for infrastructure investment has risen and is expected to grow due to many competing pressures. For example, economic growth globally and advances made through technology, along with needed investments to address climate change, urbanisation and demographic changes will require more and better designed climate resilient infrastructure investment. Infrastructure investment is a shared responsibility across levels of government, with subnational governments playing a crucial role. Many key areas of infrastructure – from water to sanitation to transportation to education – are often the responsibility of regional and local governments.

The OECD estimates that approximately USD 95 trillion in public and private investments will be needed in energy, transport, water and telecommunications infrastructure at global level between 2016 and 2030 in order to support growth and sustainable development, equivalent to approximately USD 6.3 trillion per year over the next 15 years.

Public sources of funding are insufficient to cover the investment needs in cities and regions and will remain insufficient if appropriate actions are not taken. The magnitude of the needs and the tight fiscal context for governments imply that mobilising private sources of financing will be crucial. Public Private Partnerships (PPP) could help narrow the infrastructure gap. However, PPPs are complex and sometimes risky arrangements, and there have been many examples in recent years of PPP failures or misuse, which call for caution in their use, in particular at the subnational level.

Despite a growing proportion of infrastructure services that have been delivered through PPPs in the last decade, current levels of infrastructure investment taking place through PPPs are still moderate. Most OECD countries (83%) report that between 0% and 5% of public sector infrastructure investment took place through PPPs in the last three years. IMF estimates indicate that infrastructure investment via public private partnerships is still less than a tenth of public investment in advanced economies and less than a quarter of public investment in emerging market and developing economies.

Although the average value of PPPs is generally higher at the national level, the number of PPPs is higher at the subnational level. In France, for example, subnational governments granted 79% of the *contrat de partenariat* between 2005 and 2011. In Australia, about 90% of PPPs occur at the (subnational) state level. In Germany, subnational PPPs constitute approximately 80% of PPP investment in terms of volume. In the United Kingdom, local authorities acted as the contracting authority for the majority of Private Finance Initiative (PFI) projects.

PPPs present pros and cons to the public sector. Generally, PPPs are justified when they are affordable and produce greater value for money than delivering public services or public investment through traditional means. Governments expect that private sector engagement will enhance government capacity to achieve its objectives by tapping the resources (money, technology, and knowledge) of the private sector. Gains are expected to result from benefits of risk transfer, private sector incentives, know-how and innovation. However, PPPs are not risk-free. Maximising the benefits and minimising the downsides of PPPs requires substantial public sector capacity, in particular at the subnational government level.

Subnational PPPs: overcoming the challenges

The multi-level context in which subnational PPPs occur as well as their complexity raise specific issues for successful implementation. The report highlights several considerations for using them effectively at the subnational level.

Financing subnational PPPs: watching the risks

Many of the problems reported with subnational PPPs happened because they were chosen for the wrong reasons. Subnational governments may be tempted to choose PPPs to overcome tight budgets and circumvent fiscal rules - rather than seeking value for money and affordability. These are not the right justification for a PPP, and choosing a PPP for the wrong reasons can be very risky in the long-term. PPPs create long-term ordinary liabilities for subnational governments that must be addressed. PPPs are justified when partnership represents greater value for money as compared to traditional procurement, not as a way to bypass fiscal constraints.

Once in operation, PPPs are financed by government payments (i.e. availability payments), user fees, or a combination of both – each with its pros and cons. Availability payments can place a substantial burden on subnational budgets well into the future, reducing their flexibility particularly in times of fiscal constraint. While subsidies from a higher level of government can help, as the UK case demonstrates, they should be used cautiously as they may bias the value for money assessment toward PPPs. User fees raise other issues, not the least of which is the robustness of underlying demand forecasts.

Given the complexity of PPPs and the level of capacities required to design and implement them, they should be reserved for projects of a certain size. Prior OECD work has highlighted that it is important to define a minimum project value for infrastructure being delivered through a PPP. Project development costs of PPPs are significant and are higher for smaller projects. They were estimated by the World Economic Forum to be 1-3% of total project costs for large projects (above USD 100 million) and 3-4% for smaller projects.

Intergovernmental regulatory coherence facilitates PPP use

For a PPP to be feasible, private sector actors must be able to reconcile and comply with regulations across levels of government, jurisdictions, and sectors. Private actors must navigate a myriad of regulations, which increase the administrative burden – and possibly the project cost. The experience of Virginia in the United States highlights the importance of developing a flexible and inclusive statutory framework that supports private-sector participation, accountability, and transparency without inviting political interference. Ensuring regulatory coherence across levels of government is thus critical.

Cross-jurisdictional co-ordination and economies of scale: an important factor in the use of PPPs

Infrastructure investment requires economies of scale and a match between users and geographic area. Small-scale projects that may appeal to local governments may not be appropriate for a PPP. The benefits of infrastructure are also not necessarily limited to a town, city, or even a region. Such instances can require co-ordinating investment across jurisdictional boundaries which is difficult to do. A critical issue is the ability for a number of two or more jurisdictions to enter into a binding contract with private sector actors. Horizontal co-ordination across jurisdictions can help expand the geographic coverage of the PPP, lower barriers to entry presented by small-scale projects and increase the pool of interested, qualified operators.

Administrative capacity needs are high

The technical demands associated with launching and sustaining a successful PPP are substantial. Administrative capacity needs for governments are high and not static over the life cycle of the project. Subnational governments are particularly at-risk for weak partnering capacity due to their size and available resources. Here, rural areas and smaller governments may be more vulnerable to capacity constraints than larger urban ones, although, as the French case study highlights, the latter are not immune to the challenges emerging from the complexity of PPPs. Less experienced subnational governments can face substantial asymmetries of information relative to the private sector.

Skills needed vary over the course of the project cycle. It is likely to be easier for large regions or metropolitan areas to have human resources to dedicate to a PPP project in a sustained manner over time and to benefit from arrangements that facilitate economies of scale. The availability of sufficient resources over the life of a project helps to determine whether a PPP is an appropriate strategy for a subnational government.

Governments should look to involvement of private actors, financing institutions and banks in public investment to offer more than just financing for projects. It should be a way to strengthen capacities of governments at different levels and bring expertise, through better ex-ante assessment of projects, analysis of the market and credit risks, search for economies of scale and cost-effective projects.

Political commitment and accountability

Transparency and effective procurement are central to ensuring accountability given that the complexity of PPPs can increase the risks of corruption and rent seeking. By contrast, weak capacity for value-for-money assessment and a lack of transparency may allow local or regional politicians to pursue PPPs for purposes of political expediency rather than to seek increases in efficiency or effectiveness of public service delivery. It is essential to develop a clear, transparent and stable statutory framework that supports private-sector participation, without political interference. Virginia's flexible and inclusive statutory framework that supports private sector participation while encouraging accountability and transparency emerges as a key contributor to the state's successful PPP programme, along with its rigorous project review process.

Key findings and recommendations

Not all infrastructure projects represent strong candidates for PPP procurement. The choice to use a PPP should be motivated by value for money compared to traditional procurement. Small scale projects that may appeal to local governments are not appropriate for the PPP approach. They do not necessarily represent value for money nor are they commercially viable. The promotion of PPP projects at the subnational level should be directed primarily at the larger jurisdictions and regions that already have the general fiscal and institutional capacities required, and also towards priority infrastructure sectors. Addressing the infrastructure challenges that arise in smaller jurisdictions or remote regions requires sustained public investment in order to ensure inclusive and balanced development in the country.

Recommendations

Legal and policy framework

- Create a flexible and inclusive statutory framework that supports private sector participation.
- Create PPP-specific legal arrangements with a rigorous project selection and review.
- Establish clear and transparent PPP review requirements, based on value for money, affordability, but also provisions for debt review, independent audits, and official findings of public interest.
- Ensure coherence of laws and regulations across levels of government and across subnational jurisdictions.
- Strengthen the sustainability and credibility of contracts so that they do not fall apart with new political pressures.

Financial and budgetary arrangements

- PPP proposals must demonstrate superior predicted outcomes compared to traditional public procurement alternatives.
- Minimise accounting incentives to move projects "off the budget".
- Use standard *ex-ante* evaluation instruments.
- Adopt third-party scrutiny and approval prior to tender and/or before contract signature.
- Governments should look to involvement of private actors to offer more than just financing for projects, but also as a way to strengthen capacities of governments at all levels.

PPP-supporting tools

- Establish subnational PPP units, in line ministries or at an arm's length from government.
- Provide standardised documents and examples of contracts adapted to different sectors, to dilute preparation costs and better support subnational governments in the preparation of PPPs.
- Higher levels of government may opt for advisory rather than mandatory guidance in order to minimise the risk that standardisation constrains flexibility and innovation at the subnational level.

- Develop or strengthen performance indicator systems for PPP design and implementation.
- Create peer-to-peer knowledge exchange platforms for subnational governments as well as mechanisms for inter-municipal and regional co-ordination.
- Establish national observatories/platforms to collect data and advise cities and regions in their choices to follow PPP performance.
- Collect more systematically data on subnational PPPs to fill the data gaps.

Chapter 1. A look at the challenges and governance of subnational public-private partnerships

Worldwide, infrastructure needs are substantial. Subnational governments – cities, towns, and regions - play a vital role in the infrastructure landscape. Public-private partnerships (PPPs) represent an alternative to traditional government procurement with the potential to improve value for money. However, PPPs are complex and sometimes risky arrangements that require capacity to undertake them that is not always readily available in government. This chapter offers a general framework for considering subnational public-private partnerships in a multi-level governance context. It does so by drawing on existing literature and building on recent OECD work, incorporating relevant data, and integrating examples from the three case studies included in this report: the case of PPPs in France, the case of local Private Finance Initiative (PFI) projects in the United Kingdom, and the case of PPPs in the US state of Virginia.

Introduction

Worldwide, infrastructure needs are substantial. By one estimate, the world needs to spend approximately USD 3.3 trillion annually between 2016 and 2030 on roads, bridges, ports, power plants, water facilities, and other forms of economic infrastructure just to keep up with global growth (McKinsey, 2016). The OECD estimates that around USD 95 trillion of investments will be needed between 2016 and 2030 in energy, transport, water and telecommunications infrastructure to sustain growth, or around USD 6.3 trillion per year (OECD, 2017). Subnational governments – cities, towns, and regions - play a vital role in the infrastructure landscape. Important infrastructure assets and associated services are often the sole or shared responsibility of these governments. Water services, public lighting, waste management, sanitation, public transportation, roads (Plummer, 2002; Beato and Vives, 2003) as well as health and education are often the responsibility of regional and local governments. Ports and airports may also be subnational responsibilities in some countries (Kappeler et al., 2012). But subnational governments' resources, both in terms of money and know-how, may fall short of what is needed to meet demand efficiently and effectively. Partnerships can help narrow the gap. Public-private partnerships (PPPs) represent an alternative to traditional government procurement with the potential to improve value for money. However, PPPs are complex and sometimes risky arrangements that require capacity to undertake them that is not always readily available in government.

The 2014 OECD Recommendation on Effective Public Investment Across Levels of Government helps governments to assess their public investment capacity in a multi-level governance perspective and to set priorities for improvement. The Recommendation notes the value that the private sector can bring to achieving public investment goals. At the same time, it acknowledges that careful consideration of private sector involvement includes informed consideration of subnational governments' capacity for effective engagement in public-private partnerships. Depending on the circumstance, PPPs for infrastructure investment may be under- or overused due to knowledge limitations and governance capacity constraints. Understanding key challenges and building capacity are thus important for successfully using of PPPs where they add value – and for steering subnational governments toward other modes of delivery where appropriate.

This chapter offers a general framework for considering subnational public-private partnerships in a multi-level governance context. It does so by drawing on existing literature and building on recent OECD work, incorporating relevant data, and integrating examples from the three case studies included in this report: the case of PPPs in France, the case of local Private Finance Initiative (PFI) projects in the United Kingdom, and the case of PPPs in the US state of Virginia. The chapter begins by outlining the nature of public-private partnerships and their place on the continuum of options for private sector involvement in infrastructure. Discussion then turns to the prevalence of PPPs for tackling global infrastructure challenges, with specific attention to the case of subnational governments. It then examines the challenges that public and private actors face when implementing PPPs at the subnational level. The chapter concludes with a look at how different governance arrangements can assist subnational governments in addressing the challenges raised by PPPs in a decentralised context.

PPPs: A vehicle for delivering infrastructure

Understanding PPPs

There is no single, global definition of public-private partnerships. According to the OECD (2013a:96) "public-private partnerships (PPPs) are long-term contractual agreements between the government and a private partner whereby the latter typically finances and delivers public services using a capital asset (e.g. transport or energy infrastructure, hospital or school buildings). The private party may be tasked with the design, construction, financing, operation, management and delivery of the service for a pre-determined period of time, receiving its compensation from fixed unitary payments or tolls charged to users." This definition includes both "pure" PPPs (where the main source of revenue is government payments) and concessions (where the main source of revenue is user fees) (OECD, 2013a).

PPPs fall along a continuum of approaches that involve the private sector in public service delivery and investment, and are distinguished by the degree of risk assumed by the private parties. At one end of the continuum is traditional procurement which involves some transfer of risk to the private parties but the scope is limited, does not include risks involved with service delivery (OECD, 2008), "and usually does not extend beyond the construction phase of the project" (Burger and Hawkesworth, 2011:5). At the other end of the spectrum is privatisation – the case in which the private sector assumes nearly all risk. PPPs fall between these two categories of private sector involvement. They generally combine the construction and operational aspects of infrastructure development (Burger and Hawkesworth, 2011).

The focus of this chapter is PPPs used to design, build, finance, and operate infrastructure assets. These assets contribute to "economic infrastructure" (which support economic activity and productivity such as road and rail networks, ports, public transportation, telecommunications, electricity, and water) or "social infrastructure" (which support public service delivery, such as government buildings, schools, health facilities, libraries, and social housing) (WEF, 2013). Historically, governments designed, financed, and operated these assets directly (Farrugia et al., 2008). With public-private partnerships, responsibility for assessing societal needs, setting investment objectives, approving projects, and project oversight remains with government – but private actors assume all or partial responsibility for designing, building, financing, and/or operating infrastructure assets (Farrugia et al., 2008).[1] In return for its role in a PPP, the private partner receives a stream of payments from the government, from users (user charges), or both.

PPPs present pros and cons to the public sector.[2] Generally, PPPs are justified when they are affordable[3] and produce greater value for money[4] than delivering public services or public investment through traditional means (OECD, 2008). Governments expect that private sector engagement will enhance government capacity to achieve its objectives by tapping the resources (money, technology, and knowledge) of the private sector. However, PPPs are not risk-free. As subsequent discussions will make clear, opting for PPPs exposes a government to potential downsides. These include, but are not limited to, sizeable financial obligations. Maximising the benefits and minimising the downsides of PPPs requires substantial public sector capacity.

PPPs for meeting infrastructure demand worldwide

Evaluating the role of PPPs in meeting global infrastructure demand is challenging. As there is no single definition of a PPP, there are no definitive figures regarding the number and value of these arrangements worldwide. Moreover, databases that only include projects with a minimum deal size may well omit subnational PPPs that tend to have lesser value. Figures from different sources are not comparable but instead provide a general indication of market size. Some studies (e.g. Verhoest et al., 2015; OECD, 2013a) suggest that PPPs play an important but modest part in meeting infrastructure needs. In a 2010 OECD survey of 20 countries, nine reported that PPPs constituted less than 5% of public sector infrastructure investment; seven reported the figure was somewhere between 5% and 10% (Burger and Hawkesworth, 2011). McKinsey (2016: 19) reports similar figures for "economies that make strong use" of PPPs for economic infrastructure. Looking within a sector, the Virginia case study in this report notes that PPPs accounted for approximately 2% of highway investments in the United States between 2007 and 2013.

Despite a growing proportion of infrastructure services that have been delivered through PPPs in the last decade, current levels of infrastructure investment taking place through PPPs is still moderate. Most OECD countries (83%) reported to have between 0% and 5% of public sector infrastructure investment taking place through PPPs in the last 3 years (2018 Capital Budgeting and Infrastructure Governance Survey). IMF estimates indicate that infrastructure investment via public private partnerships is still less than a tenth of public investment in advanced economies and less than a quarter of public investment in emerging market and developing economies.

PPPs are used more extensively in some parts of the world than in others. Data from different sources suggest that PPP activity tends to be greatest in Europe, followed by the Americas, Asia-Pacific, Africa and the Middle East (PWC, 2013; Public Works Financing, 2013). Low-income countries tend to lag behind their higher income counterparts in PPP uptake, as "the quality of the enabling environment, the lack of demand ... for public-private partnerships (PPPs) and capacity to handle the public-private sector interface, are all seriously impeding private sector investments. The most immediate constraint, however, remains the lack of a pipeline of technically ready and financially viable projects" (World Bank, 2011: 9). Despite these hurdles, since 1990 there has been infrastructure investment in developing countries – albeit somewhat uneven – in the form of PPPs (broadly defined). According to the World Bank (2016a: 37), between 1990 and 2014 low- and middle-income countries received USD 1.44 trillion in commitments to finance infrastructure PPPs.[5] These data show that commitments rose between 1990 and 1997, falling off sharply after the Asian financial crisis through 2005. The pattern repeated itself between 2005 and 2012, with commitments rising seven-fold to a high of USD 158 billion, but dropping off rapidly in recent years as emerging markets slowed. A significant decline occurred in 2013. Since then, however, investment commitments in PPPs have grown, albeit slowly, reflecting the overall slowdown in key emerging markets, particularly Brazil and India (World Bank, PPIAF, 2015).

PPPs at the subnational level

Global figures on the number and value of PPP deals obscure the important role of subnational governments. As noted earlier, important infrastructure assets and associated public services are often the sole or shared responsibility of cities, town, and regions. In 2014, about 59% of public investment in the OECD area occurred at the subnational level (OECD, 2016). In some countries, some of these responsibilities are relatively new - emerging as a result of decentralisation reforms that shifted greater responsibility to regional and local levels, but not always accompanied by a corresponding increase in resources (Harper and Daughters, 2007; Plummer, 2002). At the same time, globalisation has affected regional and local economies, resulting in a need for new strategies and investments for regional and local growth (OECD, 2007; Harper and Daughters, 2007).

Even if PPPs play a modest part in meeting global infrastructure needs, where they occur many are contracted subnationally. In France, between 2005 and 2011, subnational governments granted 79% of *contrat de partenariat* (CP) (EPEC, 2012a). In Germany, subnational PPPs constitute approximately 80% of PPP investment (OECD, 2013b). About 90% of PPPs in Australia occur at the (subnational) state level (EIU, 2012). In Canada, too, nearly all PPPs are contracted subnationally (Figure 1.1). In the United Kingdom, local authorities procured the majority of PFI deals, particularly school projects (Figure 1.2). According to data provided by Park (2013), in Korea, subnational governments act as the competent authority for 74% of PPPs.[6]

Figure 1.1 PPPs by sector and level of government in Canada, as of 1 May 2017

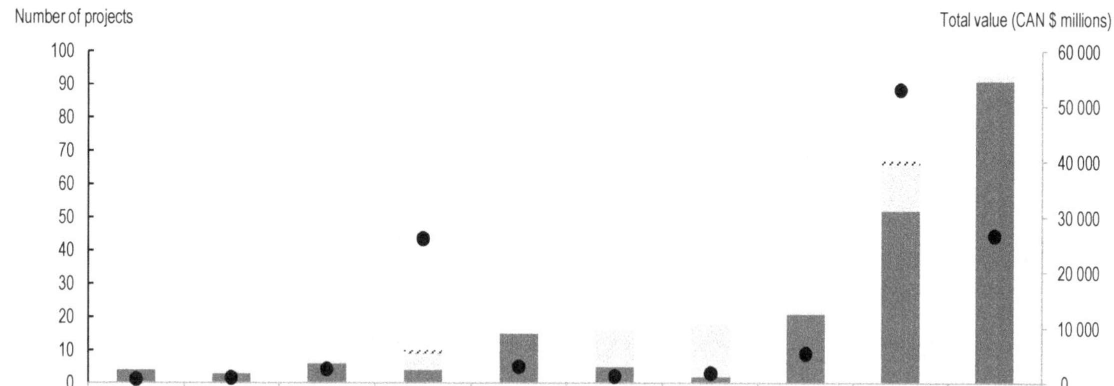

	IT	Government Services	Accomoda-tions	Energy	Education	Recreation and Culture	Water & Wastewater	Justice	Transport	Health
Other				1					1	
Municipal		1	1	5		11	16	1	14	2
Provincial	3	3	4	4	15	5	2	20	47	91
Federal	1		2					1	5	
● Total value	773	1,008	2,546	26,091	3,060	1,293	1,787	5,424	53,014	26,584

Notes: (1) Includes only costs of projects where costs have been finalised and released. (2) PPPs are at all stages of development, from RFQ/RFP to expired projects. No cancelled PPPs. (3) "Other" refers to (a) the Namgis First Nation and (b) to multiple levels of government in both the United States and Canada for a cross-border bridge project. (4) The database includes projects dating back to 1991 and includes some early projects that transferred risk from the public sector to the private sector that were considered PPPs at the time (e.g. service contracts, operations contracts, Design-Build-Own-Operate contracts) but do not fit the current definition of PPP - which requires a private sector financing component. Identified as an "other" model in the database, they are also included here.

Source: Author's elaboration based on the Canadian Council for Public-Private Partnerships (CCPPP) Project Database, http://projects.pppcouncil.ca/ (accessed 1 May 2017). Description of "other" model provided directly by the CCPPP.

Figure 1.2 PFI projects by sector and level of government in the UK,United Kingdom, as of March 2014

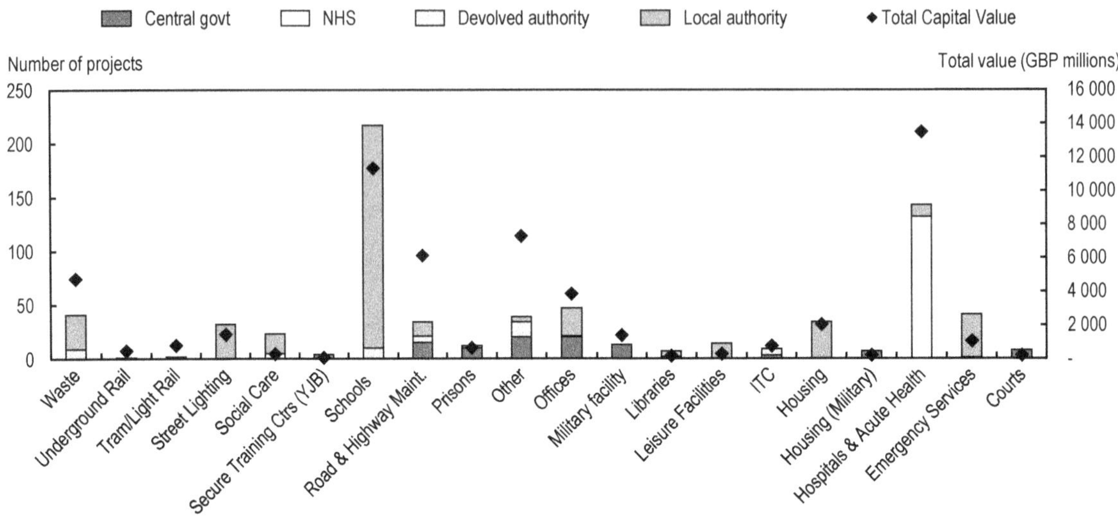

Note: Assignment to level of government is based on the "procuring authority" listed in the dataset. Current projects exclude expired or terminated projects and projects in procurement (see Mizell, 2018, this report). Here, "other" includes deals indicated as "other" in the dataset, plus two central government equipment deals and one local energy deal. "Housing" collapses HRA and non-HRA housing. "Schools" combines BSF and non-BSF projects.

Source: Author's elaboration based on HM Treasury (2014), "Current projects as at 31 March 2014", Excel.

While the total number of PPPs can be high at the subnational level, the value of individual contracts tends to be smaller than national ones. In France, the average contract value for local government CPs as of 2011 was approximately EUR 28 million versus approximately EUR 315 million for national ones (EPEC, 2012a). As the case study on the United Kingdom in this report reveals, the highest value Private Finance Initiative (PFI) contracts also tended to be awarded by the central government. The case study indicates that for current projects as of March 2014, 14% of the total number of projects was procured by the central government (with an average capital value of GBP 158.6 million).[7] By contrast, 60% of the total number of projects was procured by local authorities (with an average capital value of GBP 56.4 million). The pattern of high numbers of projects at the subnational level but lower project value is also the case for Korea (Park, 2013).

Even if subnational governments do not award the PPP contract, they can contribute to or detract from its effectiveness.[8] First, important elements of project execution, such as issuing licences or permits, may lie with subnational governments (UNCITRAL, 2001). Second, local knowledge plays an important role in tailoring capital investments to the local characteristics (Harper and Daughters, 2007). Importantly, regional and local investment needs often vary according to characteristics of the place. Globally, for example, urban needs are expected to be particularly acute. In 2014, 46% of the OECD population lived in predominantly urban regions (OECD, 2016). Developing countries face a rapidly changing, urbanising landscape. It is estimated that by 2030 about 60% of the global population will be living in cities (World Bank, 2016a). Urbanisation imposes significant infrastructure challenges for regional and local governments in areas ranging from transportation to sanitation to education.

Rural areas, in contrast to urban ones, often face declining population density making economies of scale difficult to achieve. A need for connectivity and access to markets, and the role of agriculture in the rural economy can translate into infrastructure demands that differ from urban areas.[9] Again, needs differ by level of development. Rural areas in developed countries are often saddled with aging infrastructure (see, for example, Blandford et al., 2008), while in some developing countries infrastructure for basic public services, such as clean water or electricity, may be absent or lag well behind urban areas (World Bank, 2016a; 2017). Informal connectivity to services such as water or electricity may dominate among the most poor (in both urban and rural areas). Subnational governments may be best placed to observe and respond to this dynamic when partnering for infrastructure improvements (Harper and Daughters, 2007).

Challenges to PPPs in a decentralised context

Opportunities for private participation in subnational infrastructure investment co-exist with important challenges. The challenges described here arise from the multi-level governance context in which PPPs operate and the complexities of PPPs. "Multi-level governance" refers to a "dispersion of governance across multiple jurisdictions" (Hooghe and Marks, 2010: 17) which makes the goals, authority, and capacities of numerous actors relevant for PPPs. Actors may be arranged vertically (among different levels of government) or horizontally (across jurisdictions at the same level of government).[10] Such arrangements raise issues for the successful implementation of PPPs in key areas such as financing and funding, intergovernmental regulatory coherence, and cross-jurisdictional co-ordination and economies of scale. The complexities of PPPs and the skills required to undertake them raise questions regarding administrative capacity and accountability in the public sector. These issues, raised elsewhere regarding private sector participation in infrastructure (Beato and Vives, 2003) and PPPs at the subnational level (Harper and Daughters, 2007), echo the challenges of implementing public policy in a multi-level governance context generally (Charbit and Michalun, 2009; OECD, 2009a). Left unaddressed, they represent potential obstacles to successful PPPs. This section discusses the key challenges for PPPs in a multi-level governance context.

Financing and funding

A key domain in which multi-level governance matters for subnational PPPs is the financial one. The specific circumstances of subnational governments can affect the decision to enter into a PPP, the approach to (and cost of) financing a PPP, and the eventual payment for infrastructure availability and use.

Choosing a PPP

Decentralisation arrangements can lead to costly subnational responsibilities for which own resources are not enough. Subnational government often tap (and in some cases rely on) intergovernmental transfers to meet spending obligations. But resources may still be insufficient to accommodate needs for infrastructure development, operation, and maintenance without borrowing. In many cases, subnational governments often face important borrowing constraints (e.g. borrowing limits, weaker credit). Public-private partnerships can appeal to governments looking to work around these fiscal constraints.

Opting for PPPs in order to overcome tight budgets and circumvent fiscal rules - rather than seeking value for money and affordability - is not the right justification for a PPP, but it can be appealing. In the short-term, the private partner is usually responsible for the capital expenditure, enabling a government to develop capital assets without paying for them immediately. The cost of infrastructure shifts to the future, potentially to a next generation of taxpayers, and beyond the electoral cycle of politicians (Musson, 2009). Fiscal constraints can thus create an incentive to use PPPs and in some cases to move investment "off the books". However, risks to this approach are high.

PPPs create long-term ordinary liabilities for subnational governments that must be addressed and, depending on their design, contingent liabilities that must be accounted for lest they create fiscal risks. For example, in the United Kingdom until recently PPPs often took the form of "Private Finance Initiative" (PFI) contracts procured by local authorities, NHS Trusts, or central government departments (HM Treasury, 2012).[11] As of March 2014, there were 728 current projects with a capital value of GBP 56.6 billion (HM Treasury, 2014b). Total PFI unitary charge payments for 2015-16 were expected to amount to GBP 10.5 billion (HM Treasury, 2014b). In some cases, poor financial management and procurement of PFIs have left English NHS trusts in a precarious financial state (Mathieson, 2014).

Given a political willingness to consider private sector engagement, the decision to enter into a PPP involves substantial ex-ante analysis regarding the costs and benefits of PPPs, as compared to traditional procurement, over the life cycle of the asset. As recommended by the OECD Principles for Public Governance of PPPs, it is essential to "carefully investigate which investment method is likely to yield most value for money. Key risk factors and characteristics of specific projects should be evaluated by conducting a procurement option pre-test. A procurement option pre-test should enable the government to decide on whether it is prudent to investigate a Public-Private Partnerships option further" (OECD, 2012).

The technical capacity required for this analysis can be substantial, placing demands on a subnational government's administrative capacities. As later discussion reveals, weak subnational administrative capacity can be problematic in the case of PPPs and will need to be reinforced in order to ensure that the decision to enter into a PPP is based not on a short-term desire to bypass fiscal constraints, but rather on accurate assessment of the lifecycle specificities of a given project.

Financing PPPs at the subnational level

A second financial concern for PPPs at the subnational level involves their financing. PPP financing often flows through a Special Purpose Vehicle (SPV) (Moszoro and Gasiorowski, 2008) in the form of non-recourse (or limited recourse) project financing. In this case, lenders and investors rely on the revenue generated by the PPP project to repay debts and earn a return on their investments (see Box 1.1). PPP design therefore matters greatly to ensure sufficient revenue once the asset is in operation. As debt makes up the majority of financing, access to credit is crucial – but subnational projects may find it more difficult to access credit than the national projects with which they may have to compete (von Thadden, 2012). "Non-recourse" debt tends to be high risk and as subnational credit ratings can be lower than that of national governments, debt costs can be higher (reflecting concerns that a subnational government may fail to meet its financial obligations). This in turn raises the issue of sub-sovereign guarantees (von Thadden, 2012). Such guarantees, in which the national government (or financial institutions) backstop subnational financial obligations either through "soft" or "hard" commitments can help to mitigate creditor payment risk, lower debt pricing, and strengthen value for money (EPEC, 2011). However, they can also encourage less-than-robust decision-making due to the belief that losses will bailed out by the national government.

While the private partner generally makes the initial capital investment for the PPP, the public partner may contribute as well (see Box 1.1).[12] One form of support is capital grants. These grants can lower the necessary private sector capital expenditures and in turn reduce future payments made to the private partner (PPIAF and PWC, 2006). While some well-off subnational governments may have the ability to make a direct financial contribution themselves, capital grants often come from a higher level of government (which can make subnational PPPs subject to the rules and priorities of higher levels of government). In some cases, subnational PPPs have a hard time getting financing, even in the form of government support, due to their size. Commercial banks may be unwilling to lend without some form of government support, but such support may be available only for projects larger than a given threshold. A small project, such as a local water project, may thus go to market with very high rates of equity financing.[13]

Paying for PPPs at the subnational level

The third financial challenge for subnational governments involves paying for PPPs over the long-term. Private partners generally recoup their investment through a fee paid by the government partner, user-fees, or a combination of both. Government payments, for example, can be "availability payments" (based on asset availability at contractually defined specifications) or "shadow tolls" (payments/subsidy per unit of service) (World Bank Institute and PPIAF, 2012). Even where user-fees play an important role, a government (and perhaps even a higher level of government) may still find itself facing a financial obligation, for example if it made a "minimum revenue guarantee" and demand proves weaker than expected. In 2013, 90% of the PPPs reaching financial close in Europe involved availability payments; only six involved user fees (EPEC, 2014). The three case studies demonstrate a mix of payment models: PFIs in the United Kingdom relied on availability payments and Virginia's transportation PPPs rely on tolling and direct government payments. France has a long history of concessions, which rely on user fees, but has more recently introduced PPPs using availability payments. With respect to government payments, concern relates to the subnational government's ability to pay for the ordinary (and possibly contingent) liabilities discussed earlier. This involves a subnational government's capacity to generate and have available revenue to cover its financial obligations to the private partners. Here, parties face issues regarding subnational expenditure and revenue assignment, tax autonomy (and fiscal rules), the efficiency of revenue collection, the availability of intergovernmental transfers to finance ordinary liabilities for PPPs, and overall financial management practices.[14] Subnational governments also face a so-called "surprise risk" resulting from a policy shift at the national level that affects their ability to meet their contractual obligations.[15] This might include, for example, policy changes that affect service pricing or the allocations of public funds to make availability payments (Saragiotis, 2009). According to the UK case study, the national government made funds available to English local authorities to help cover the cost of unitary charges for PFI projects. These "PFI credits" were a central feature of many local projects but were discontinued in 2010 as they were seen to create a bias toward PFI when evaluating procurement alternatives.

Box 1.1. Basic principles of project finance for PPPs

Infrastructure PPPs frequently operate through a Special Purpose Vehicle (SPV), a legal entity set up to undertake the PPP project. Financing flows through the SPV generally in the form of "project finance", in which lenders and investors rely entirely ("non-recourse" financing) or mainly ("limited recourse" financing) on the cash flow generated by the project to repay debts and earn a return on their investments.

Project finance comes from three main sources. Debt provided by lenders or capital market investors can be raised via bank loans, bond issuance, and multi-lateral agency/development bank loans. "Senior debt", which gets priority in terms of repayment, usually constitutes 70-80% of financing. The financing structure may also include other forms of junior (subordinated) debt (e.g. "mezzanine" debt) which ranks between senior debt and pure equity in terms of repayment. Equity generally constitutes 20-30% of project financing. Equity comes from project sponsors, as well as contractors, financial institutions, and in some cases, government. A large part of the equity may be shareholder subordinated debt (shareholder loans) because the interest is tax deductible. Equity investors bear the primary risks in PPP financing and therefore demand a higher return on the funds they provide. Finally, PPP financing may also benefit from government support in order to attract financing and/or make them more affordable.

Finally, PPPs may involve credit enhancements to reduce the cost of debt and mitigate certain risks. As noted, some credit enhancements may come from government (see Table 1 below). Others may come from the sponsors and/or third parties. These can include: guarantees relating to the performance of the SPV or other participants' contractual obligations; financing facilities that offer temporary liquidity to address specific risks (e.g. local currency depreciation); and insurance against certain project related risks (e.g. construction risks, loss of revenue, third party liability, environmental liability).

Sources: EPEC (2012), "Project Finance" in "The Guide to Guidance: How to Prepare, Procure and Deliver PPP Projects", European PPP Expertise Centre, wwwwww.eib.org/epec/g2g/annex/1-project-finance (accessed 22 January 2014); World Bank (2016), "Government Support in Financing PPPs" (last updated 8 September 2016) and "Risk Mitigation Mechanisms" (last updated 31 October 2016), The Public-Private Partnership in Infrastructure Resource Center (PPPIRC), http://ppp.worldbank.org/public-private-partnership/financing (accessed 12 May 2017); Infrastructure Concession Regulatory Commission (2012),"6.4 Sources of Finance" in "PPP Manual for Nigeria"; PPIAF & PWC (2006), "Hybrid PPPs: Levering EU Funds and Private Capital", January, wwwwww.irfnet.ch/files-upload/knowledges/PWC_HybridPPPs_2006.pdf; Farlex Financial Dictionary, (2012), "Take-Out Commitment", http://financial-dictionary.thefreedictionary.com/Take+Out+Financing (accessed 9 December 2013); Yescombe, E. (2013), Principles of Project Finance, 2nd Edition, Academic Press, GoogleBooks.

Table 1.1. Key instruments of government support for PPP project finance

DIRECT SUPPORT	
Grants	The government may offer *direct financial assistance* to defray construction costs, to procure land, to provide assets, to compensate for bid costs, etc.
In-kind support	The government may offer *in-kind support*, e.g. waiving fees, costs and other payments that the private sector would otherwise need to pay to a public entity.
Equity	The government may be an equity investor in the SPV.
Debt	The government may provide loans.
Shadow tolls/ tariff subsidies	The government may pay shadow tolls for roads or top-up tariff payments.
CONTINGENT PRODUCTS	
Guarantees	The government may provide guarantees such as for debt, exchange rates, currency convertibility, demand for services (e.g. toll revenue), etc.
Indemnities	The government may agree to compensate the private actors in the event of non-payment by state entities, such as for revenue shortfall or cost overruns.
Insurance	The government may act as an insurer of last resort if certain risks (e.g. terrorism, force majeure, etc.) are otherwise uninsurable.
Hedging	The government may participate in hedging mechanisms to hedge against certain risks (e.g. currency exchange rates, interest rates or commodity pricing).
Contingent debt	The government may promise to lend money under different scenarios such as *take-out financing* (if the project can only obtain short-term debt, the government promises to loan funds at a given interest rate at a certain date in the future) or *revenue support* (a commitment to lend money to the project company to make up for revenue short falls in order to satisfy debt-service obligations).

Note: The World Bank includes intermediation of debt from commercial financial markets and project development funding as two other forms of government support for PPPs.
Source: Adapted from World Bank (2016), "Government Support in Financing PPPs".

Where user-fees are involved, subnational governments must consider how they will be implemented, with an appropriately designed and regulated pricing policy. In many countries, governments subsidise consumer use of infrastructure. As Beato and Vives (2003) note, transitioning to private provision of infrastructure can mean an increase in user fees, which may be highly unpopular with consumers. They highlight that public discontent with user fees can raise political issues and risks that may discourage private participation.[16] Government subsidies may need to continue if consumers have a low ability to pay for services (Beato and Vives, 2003; WEF, 2012), again raising issues of the availability of public funds. A discussion of public objection to tolls for transportation projects can be found in the case study of Virginia (this report). The state has subsidised some tolls to promote policy priorities, such as carpooling (see Box 1.2).

Finally, launching a PPP involves costs for feasibility studies, contract design, and other project development requirements. According to the World Economic Forum (2013), for large (> USD 500 million) and medium-sized (> USD 100 million) projects, such costs may be 1-3% of total project costs. For smaller projects, the figures range from 3-4% of total costs, making infrastructure PPPs cost-effective only after they reach a certain size (WEF, 2013). Some countries have established independent project development funds or facilities to help cover these costs (World Bank, 2016c).

Box 1.2. Mixing tolls and subsidies to promote public priorities in the US state of Virginia

"Virginia's PPP programme works to develop public-interest projects that remain sufficiently attractive for private investment, even when public policy diverges from private-sector interests. For example, state policy encourages carpooling, typically exempting high occupancy vehicles (HOV) from tolls to the disadvantage of toll-collecting concessionaires. To accommodate both HOV policy and private financial viability, several Virginian PPP concession agreements include provisions ensuring lost-revenue compensation for concessionaires if/when HOV traffic exceeds a pre-determined rate. According to the I-95 Express Lanes agreement, for example, the state will pay 70% of the average toll for HOV vehicles exceeding 35-38% of total traffic flow (Virginia Department of Transportation, 2012: 13–14). For the first two quarters of operation in 2015, HOV traffic accounted for 32% of all traffic in these lanes, approaching the compensation threshold (Shenk, 2015a; 2015b). The 495 Express Lanes agreement includes a similar provision for HOV vehicles exceeding 24% of total traffic flow (Virginia Department of Transportation, 2007). Such provisions offer a mechanism to accommodate both public and private sector interests to produce a mutually beneficial project."

Source: Quote from Gifford, J. and M. Transue (2018), "Public-Private Partnerships for Infrastructure at the Subnational Level of Government: Opportunities and Challenges in the Commonwealth of Virginia", Chapter 4 of this report. The authors cite Virginia Department of Transportation (2012), "Comprehensive Agreement Relating to the I-95 HOV/HOT Lanes Project"; Shenk, S. (2015a), "I-95 Tolls Bring in $9 Million in First Quarter", Fredericksburg.com, 25 April, www.fredericksburg.com/news/transportation/i--tolls-bring-in-million-in-first-quarter/article_c198630e-fe30-5d82-bc37-9fe4e0929232.html, Shenk, S. (2015b), "I-95 Express Lanes Continue to Rake in the Money, Ringing up $15 Million in the Second Quarter", Fredericksburg.com, 11 July, www.fredericksburg.com/news/transportation/i--express-lanes-continue-to-rake-in-the-money/article_4913b520-593e-533e-8bb4-f1198c2ae7f5.html, Virginia Department of Transportation (2007), "Amended and Restated Comprehensive Agreement Relating to the Route 495 HOT Lanes in Virginia Project".

Intergovernmental regulatory coherence

A second domain in which multi-level governance has a notable impact for PPPs is regulation.[17] For a PPP to be feasible, private sector actors must be able to reconcile and comply with regulations at different levels of government, across sectors, and across fields of law (WEF, 2013). Complications emerge because legislation authorising the creation of PPPs and associated enabling regulations can exist at multiple levels of government. Depending on the country:

> *... privately financed infrastructure projects may require the involvement of several public authorities, at various levels of government. For instance, the competence to lay down regulations and rules for the activity concerned may rest in whole or in part with a public authority at a level different from the one that is responsible for providing the relevant service. It may also be that both the regulatory and the operational functions are combined in one entity, but that the authority to award government contracts is centralised in a different public authority. For projects involving foreign investment, it may also happen that certain specific competences*

fall within the mandate of an agency responsible for approving foreign investment proposals. (UNCITRAL, 2001: 28-29)

Responsibility for issuing "licences and permits that may be needed in the course of a project" may be distributed across levels of government and agencies at the same level of government as well (UNCITRAL, 2001: 30).[18]

While subnational governments may have the authority to enter into PPP contract, laws and regulations at higher levels of government can constrain how they may do so. A Canadian municipality considering PPPs, for example, must determine if its authority to engage in a PPP is constrained by laws and regulations of the provincial or national government, if regulatory changes are required, and if this assessment differs across sectors and asset classes (Canadian Council for Public-Private Partnerships, 2011).[19] For European Union countries, national and subnational governments must take account of supra-national requirements, such as the EU's procurement directive and directive on concession contracts (EC, 2014a; 2014b). The EU further regulates whether or not a given PPP should be considered "on or off-balance sheet", which has implications for the public partner's financing of the PPP (Petersen, 2011). PPPs that cross administrative boundaries may need to take account of the legal and regulatory environment in more than one country or region (e.g. in federal countries).

Examples of regulatory difficulties are not difficult to find. By one assessment, the PPP market in the United States, particularly for transportation projects, is not unlike "50 different countries" (Partnerships Bulletin, 2012: 5). The federal government has facilitated the use of PPPs through national legislation, federal guidance, innovative financing mechanisms, experimental pilot programmes, and information sharing (Rall et al., 2010). At the same time individual states promulgate their own statutes for PPPs (Rall et al., 2010; Istrate and Puentes, 2011; Richardson, 2010) – which affect not only what happens at the state level, but at the local level as well. This legislation varies in terms of sectoral coverage, permissible payment schemes, treatment of unsolicited proposals, use of non-compete clauses, the authority of lower level agencies, such as metropolitan transit authorities, to enter into PPPs and more (Istrate and Puentes, 2011). (See also a discussion of the US PPP market in the Virginia case study, this report). Another example comes from Brazil, where one assessment of the PPP market was generally positive but noted important challenges arising from "multiple legal frameworks between the states" (Partnerships Bulletin, 2012). While the Economist Intelligence Unit (2013a) found the overall institutional arrangements in Brazil to be generally coherent (vertically) across levels of government, it also highlighted the (horizontal) heterogeneity across states.[20]

Cross-jurisdictional co-ordination and economies of scale

Infrastructure investment often requires economies of scale. Moreover, the benefits of infrastructure investment are often not limited to a city or town, or sometimes even a region. Such instances can require co-ordinating investment across regional or municipal boundaries (Beato and Vives, 2003). Co-ordination can be beneficial for achieving economies of scale, for addressing spillovers, for encouraging synergies, and for ensuring that investments in neighbouring or otherwise linked jurisdictions do not work at cross-purposes (OECD, 2014; Mizell and Allain-Dupré, 2013). This is increasingly important in the face of the global trend toward urbanisation. Functional urban areas cover multiple municipalities (see Figure 1.3.). However, even a large metropolitan area may not fully capture the geographic boundaries of a PPP. An assessment of transportation PPPs in the 100 largest US metropolitan areas found that six projects covered multiple areas. The

Indiana Toll Road, for example, crosses seven counties – two in the Chicago metropolitan area, three in smaller metro areas, and two counties in non-metropolitan areas (Istrate and Puentes, 2011).

Figure 1.3. Administrative fragmentation of metropolitan areas in OECD countries, 2014

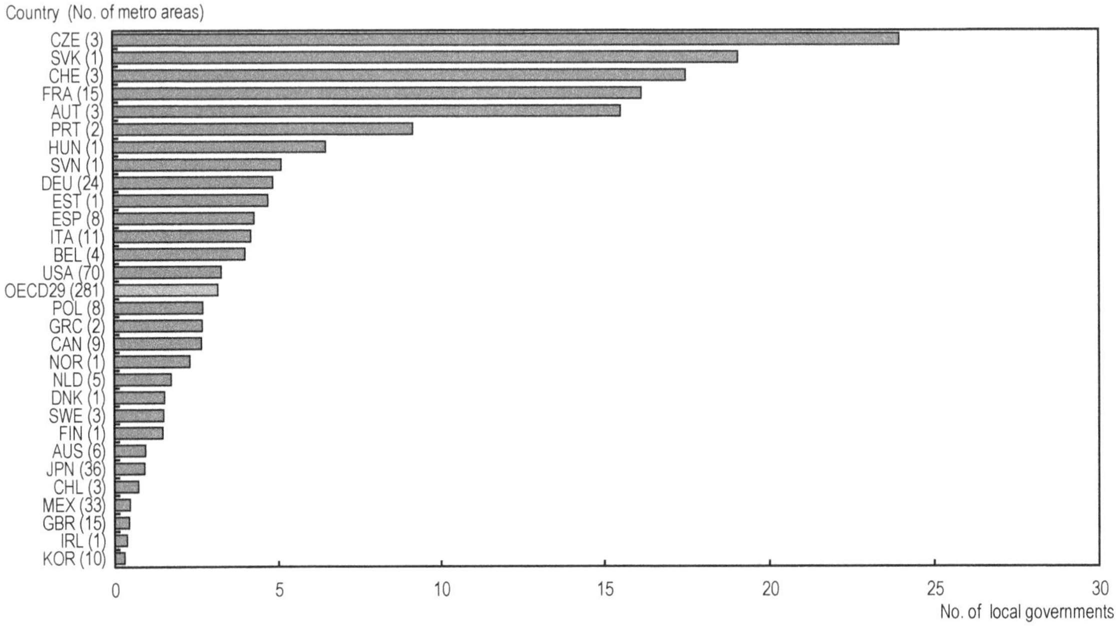

Note: Metropolitan areas are functional urban areas (FUAs) with populations exceeding 500 000 people. The OECD-EU definition of FUAs is not applied to Iceland, Israel, New Zealand and Turkey. The FUA of Luxembourg does not appear as its population is below 500 000 inhabitants. No. of local governments is circa 2011. Metropolitan population figures are estimates based on municipal figures for the last two censuses available for each country.

Source: "Figure 2.9: Administrative fragmentation of metropolitan areas, 2014" in OECD (2016), *Regions at a Glance 2016*, OECD Publishing, pg. 53, http://dx.doi.org/10.1787/reg_glance-2016-en.

By expanding the geographic coverage for investment, horizontal co-ordination can also help overcome barriers to entry presented by small-scale projects (Musson, 2009) and a lack of qualified operators to undertake them (Beato and Vives, 2003). As Beato and Vives (2003) note, large (possibly international) infrastructure operators are less likely to find small subnational projects appealing due to the costs of establishing the PPP. Horizontal co-ordination across subnational jurisdictions may attract more qualified operators to a bidding process by increasing the size (and appeal) of the contract (Beato and Vives, 2003). Subnational governments in rural areas in particular may find that they are too small, have too little capacity, and/or face a dearth of competition to structure PPPs on their own.

Although co-ordination across jurisdictions at the subnational level is valuable, it is not always easy to do. Municipalities or regions need to work together and private sector counterparts need to work with them. While the case for such co-ordination may be clear, it can be hampered by differing political agendas (Beato and Vives, 2003), differing policy priorities, resource constraints, concerns regarding the distribution of costs or benefits from co-ordinated investment (OECD, 2014), or differing constituents' views on private sector participation in public services. The structure of cross-jurisdictional collaboration for PPPs can also be complicated by issues regarding the extent to which different parties would be responsible for any contingent liabilities or termination payments in the event of failure.[21] By one account, "US state and metro areas have been relatively slow to pursue public-private partnerships, in large part because of the complexity of deals that include multiple jurisdictions, companies, and even countries" (Brookings Institution, 2012).

Administrative capacity

The technical demands associated with launching and sustaining a successful PPP are substantial (see, for example Joost and Levitt, 2009; WEF, 2013; Plummer, 2002; Harper and Daughters, 2007; Dutz et al., 2006). Not only must administrators understand the pros and cons of PPPs, and evaluate if and how to integrate their use into development plans, but they must have or be able to access the technical skills to evaluate and work with potential private partners, assess and assign risk, design a contract, and monitor (and respond to) project implementation. In many of these areas, subnational governments (particularly those with limited PPP experience, weak administrative capacity, or limited resources) may be at a disadvantage relative to the private sector. In fact, failure to bring PPPs to fruition, particularly in developing countries, is often due to a "project preparation gap", a lack of well-prepared projects that reassure the private sector in terms of their "commercial and technical feasibility, the risk allocation, the public sector's contractual commitment and capacity as well as the institutional and legal framework" (WEF, 2013: 8). Projects may suffer from delays, long preparation phases, costly due diligence for the private sector, cost overruns, and renegotiation due to poor project preparation (WEF, 2013). In addition, given the fact that subnational governments are less likely to accumulate a critical mass of projects over time, central governments should consider ways of leveraging its management capacity regarding PPPs to the benefit of subnational governments (OECD, 2012). The case study of PPPs in France focuses precisely on the challenges presented by the complexity of PPPs and the administrative capacity needed to launch and sustain them.

Bolstering public sector capacity is thus crucial for strengthening partnership activities. Unfortunately with respect to administrative capacity governments, particularly subnational ones, may find it difficult to recruit and/or retain sufficiently qualified staff (Mizell and Allain-Dupré, 2013; Harper and Daughters, 2007; Beato and Vives, 2003; OECD, 2014), especially in developing countries (WEF, 2013). Some subnational governments, such as large regions or metropolitan areas, may have sufficient human resources to dedicate to a PPP project in a sustained manner over time. Small and/or rural subnational governments, by contrast, may not (Harper and Daughters, 2007). The capacity gap between rural localities and large metropolitan areas can be substantial. Asymmetrical capacities between small local governments and large contracting companies can disadvantage subnational governments, a concern raised by the 2014 report on public-private partnerships by the French Senate (Sénat, 2014). While subnational capacity is frequently a hurdle for effective PPPs, it is worth noting that in some countries (e.g. Slovenia, Russia, Latvia, Bosnia Herzegovina) the capacity for PPPs, even if small scale ones, can be better subnationally than nationally (EIU, 2013c).

The availability of sufficient resources over the life of a project helps to determine whether a PPP is an appropriate strategy for a subnational government (Canadian Council for Public-Private Partnerships, 2011). This said, not all subnational governments need to possess the full range of technical skills in-house. Access to external specialists can help fill technical gaps[22] (Plummer, 2002), but core skills must exist in the public sector to capitalise on what PPPs offer (World Bank, 2006; Harper and Daughters, 2007) and adequately monitor private sector performance. Crucial is sufficient procurement capacity. The OECD reports that "the most prominent weakness of procurement systems identified by almost half of OECD member countries is the lack of adequate capability, both in terms of shortage of procurement officials and the insufficient specialised knowledge of available technologies, innovations or market developments" (OECD, 2013a: 134). The situation is likely exacerbated for subnational governments.

Political commitment and accountability

PPPs at the subnational level may prompt concerns regarding political commitment, accountability, and integrity. First, sustained and stable political commitment to (proper) use of PPPs is crucial to launch and sustain reforms, encourage investor confidence, and develop partnerships (WEF, 2013; World Bank, 2007; Harper and Daughters, 2007; Plummer, 2002). This point is echoed in the case study of France. However, differing political commitment to PPPs at different levels of government could potentially leave subnational governments (and the private sector) vulnerable to a shift away from supportive institutional arrangements for PPPs. Second, even if political commitment to PPPs exists, weak capacity to properly assess projects may allow local or regional politicians to pursue PPPs for political reasons rather than to improve the efficiency or effectiveness of public service delivery. Third, as noted in the French case study, the size and complexity PPPs can increase the risks of corruption and rent seeking. Public procurement, for example, is an acknowledged high-risk area for corruption. The complexity of PPPs can potentially weaken transparency and oversight in this area. As an example, in examining the environment for PPPs in Mexico, the Economist Intelligence Unit (2013b) noted efforts to strengthen PPP capacity at the subnational level. Yet, it also found, with respect to private participation in water infrastructure:[23]

> *Decisions are typically influenced by politics, tariffs do not cover the cost of conserving water systems, and the dynamics for private-sector participation remain complicated. At the municipal level, the degree of transparency when private-sector participants are involved is low. Indeed, in many cases projects are negotiated with the private sector, and the municipal councils do not exercise an adequate supervisory role. Contract changes are common, but without safeguards for equity or transparency. In the case of water services, the resolution system depends on the terms of each contract. If a municipality enters a concession directly, disputes are resolved by tribunals. However, most water PPP projects are contracted by municipal companies, which have the power to establish ad hoc arbitration schemes. Processes are not competitive and contract award criteria are highly subjective. (EIU, 2013b)*

Finally, weak capacity of subnational governments to narrow information gaps with the private sector as well as low levels of competition in the PPP market (such as in rural areas) can leave subnational governments dependent on a single or handful of private partners, vulnerable to capture, and/or open to post-award renegotiation where they may find themselves at a disadvantage.

Supporting subnational capacity for PPPs

How might governments support subnational implementation of public-private partnerships? Practitioner literature (e.g. UNECE, 2008; OECD, 2012) makes a case for "good governance" of PPPs, with specific attention to formal institutional arrangements that strengthen their quality and the administrative capacity to undertake them. This literature covers multiple dimensions such as political and policy commitment, regulatory frameworks, budgetary rules, institutional arrangements, and administrative tools. This guidance generally has a national orientation. What is often missing is a comprehensive discussion of how different mechanisms can be employed to address the challenges that subnational PPPs present. This section aims to narrow this gap in the literature by reviewing some of the tools available to policy makers and practitioners, considering how these measures could address PPPs in a decentralised context. To do this, it uses the categorisation of measures proposed by Verhoest et al. (2015) as a jumping off point, adding some measures that the authors did not include. The authors cluster different mechanisms into three categories[24]: 1) Policy and political commitment, 2) Legal and regulatory framework, and 3) PPP-supporting bodies – to which this discussion adds 4) Financial support and budgetary arrangements.

Policy and political commitment

As the previous discussion made clear, a lack of political commitment can hamper efforts to launch and sustain a PPP programme. Verhoest et al. (2015) identify three measures of "policy and political commitment": stable, articulated support from political parties, the existence of an up-to-date PPP policy document, and/or presence of PPP programme. For all levels of government, political commitment and a clear policy framework are important for defining PPPs as an alternative to traditional procurement, articulating the framework within which PPPs should occur, and "directing and coordinating cooperation between interested sectors and government institutions" (Verhoest et al., 2015). 5) Political leadership helps ensure public awareness of the trade-offs associated with PPPs, which is a key ingredient for successful stakeholder consultation and engagement throughout the investment cycle (OECD, 2012). Stakeholder engagement and transparent processes are important for clarifying the expected benefits of the project, promoting accountability, and addressing third party concerns.

For subnational governments, clear policies at the central level can illuminate higher-level priorities, help direct support to lower levels, buoy the confidence of private sector (Harper and Daughters, 2007) and reinforce policy coherence across levels of government. For example, in Australia the national and subnational governments work co-operatively through the National Public Private Partnership Forum and more specifically through its PPP Working Group to ensure policy coherence across levels of government. The Working Group spurred development of the National PPP Policy and Guidelines, prepared by Infrastructure Australia and endorsed by the Council of Australia Governments in 2008 (Infrastructure Australia, 2008; 2014).

Legal and regulatory framework

The legal and regulatory framework within which subnational PPPs occur can be enabling or disabling, depending on its complexity, comprehensiveness, and degree of coherence across levels of government. Proper legislation can improve government capacity for standardised, favourable, and transparent treatment of PPPs, as well as appropriate treatment of unsolicited proposals. In doing so, it can make private participation more appealing to private partners and to potential creditors (Richardson, 2010). For Verhoest et al. (2015: 5), "this dimension relates to the presence and context of a specifically stipulated legal framework for PPP (sic), and relevant provisions in PPP-related and public procurement regulation." PPP-specific legal arrangements can help clarify how PPPs are to be implemented (e.g. eligible sectors, roles and responsibilities, payment mechanisms, dispute resolution procedures), whereas laws and related regulations introduced without PPPs in mind can leave practitioners unclear on important aspects of implementation

(Dutz et al., 2006). According to the case study on the Commonwealth of Virginia, the state's flexible statutory framework "supports private sector participation, accountability, and transparency without inviting political interference" and "presents few barriers to entry for private parties."

However, the mere presence of PPP-specific laws and regulations is insufficient for supporting subnational PPPs. As noted earlier, the coherence of these laws and regulations across levels of government, and across subnational jurisdictions, deserves attention. Looking internationally, in 2014 the EU reformed or introduced directives on public procurement (2014/24/EU and 2014/25/EU) and concession contracts (2014/23/EU), partially in response to the heterogeneity or absence of key legislation in member countries. For example, with respect to concessions, a Commission assessment found that "the rules and practices of Member States concerning the award of concessions are very different… the principles of the Treaty are not understood and applied in the same way everywhere … [and] many EU Member States do not have rules on concessions at all" (EC, 2014a). With respect to procurement, local and regional authorities should benefit from simplified procedures and flexibility associated with the revised directives (EC, 2014b). National efforts to improve coherence include Colombia's 2012 PPP law, which introduced "obligatory procedures at national, regional and local levels for preparing PPP projects", a move expected to "improve general coordination and processes for projects at all levels of government" (EIU, 2013a: 14).

PPP-supporting tools

Verhoest et al. (2015) cluster a handful of supportive mechanisms into the category "PPP-supporting bodies". However, existing literature makes numerous recommendations for strengthening PPP design, financing, and implementation via mechanisms that are not restricted to "bodies" and are, perhaps, better described as "tools".

"PPP units" are seen as a useful way to bolster government capacity to structure and implement PPPs (see Box 1.3). Generally viewed as a "good practice" for PPP programmes (UNECE, 2008), PPP units are dedicated public entities that can act as a comprehensive tool for strengthening capacity. Most, but not all, PPP units are national, often located in a cross-sectoral ministry, such as a ministry of finance or planning. PPP units can also exist in line ministries or at an arms-length from government (Dutz et al., 2006; OECD, 2010). The role of a national PPP unit with respect to subnational governments will depend on intergovernmental fiscal and legal relations (Dutz et al., 2006). While most PPP units are national, numerous countries have units at the subnational level. In federal countries they are often established at the regional (state/provincial) level and often pre-date a national unit (OECD, 2010). They may also exist at both levels of government. The Virginia case study describes the value of the Virginia Office of Public-Private Partnerships, which develops and implements transportation PPPs. In the United Kingdom and France, PPP units have evolved or been incorporated into entities with a broader remit (see Box 1.3 and the UK case study).

Figure 1.4. The role of national PPP units to strengthen the capacities of subnational governments

Do national PPP units or Infrastructure units in central governments strengthen the capacities of subnational governments (municipalities, regions, states) to design and run PPP or infrastructure projects in general?

Yes	No
Australia	Austria
Czech Republic*	Belgium
France	Chile
Germany	Denmark
Ireland*	Estonia
Italy	Finland
Korea	Hungary
Spain	Japan
Turkey*	Luxembourg
United Kingdom	New Zealand
	Norway
	Slovenia
Non-OECD	Sweden
Philippines	Switzerland
South Africa	Mexico**

Note: Total respondents: 26; * without a mandate, ** not answered

Source: OECD Survey of Infrastructure Governance (2016).

Box 1.3. PPP units: A comprehensive tool

The specific role that PPP units play in supporting subnational capacity for PPPs will depend on the functions the PPP units undertake. PPP units tend to perform some combination of five main functions: policy formulation and co-ordination, gate keeping and quality control, technical assistance, education and capacity development, and PPP promotion (OECD, 2010; Istrate and Puentes, 2011). Each can contribute to the challenges presented by subnational PPPs.

A PPP unit can assist with intergovernmental regulatory and policy coherence by helping to clarify and streamline the legal interface that private actors confront when considering PPPs. Technical assistance can bolster the quality of the tendering process and contract documents, strengthening the position of the public sector in negotiating with private sector counterparts. By developing and encouraging the use of standardised documents and processes, a PPP unit can also help reduce transaction costs for both public and private partners (World Bank, 2006; Istrate and Puentes, 2011). A PPP unit can share information regarding good practices, opportunities, and challenges to address. Employed horizontally, this function can bridge silos, transferring lessons and experiences across sectors (World Bank, 2006) and among subnational governments. Employed vertically, information sharing can narrow knowledge gaps between levels of government.

PPP units can also address some financial challenges subnational governments confront with PPPs. Regarding the decision to enter into a partnership, a PPP unit can play a quality control function, acting as an early reviewer of PPP project proposals and ensuring that a PPP's fiscal impact is clear (Istrate and Puentes, 2011). South Africa's PPP Unit was created, at least in part, to address budgetary concerns regarding PPPs (Istrate and Puentes, 2011; World Bank, 2007). In addition to technical assistance for contract preparation and risk allocation, some PPP units channel financial support for project development costs or to cover subnational governments' financial contribution to PPPs.

In Portugal, a special unit of the Ministry of Finance (UTAP, *Unidade Técnica de Acompanhamento de Projetos*) has been since 2012 in charge of the renegotiation process of central government PPPs but also, since 2016, provides technical assistance to and monitors all PPPs, including municipal ones.

The major contribution of PPP units to subnational governments is to bolster their administrative capabilities. For large urban areas they can help negotiate complex infrastructure projects. Likewise they can backstop capacity in smaller municipalities that encounter PPPs infrequently and have little opportunity to learn by doing. PPP units can support the planning stage by helping to determine which services to expose to private participation, supporting value for money assessment to determine when a PPP is the most appropriate delivery mode, and understanding a PPP's fiscal implications. At the implementation phase, PPP units can narrow gaps in technical capacity among subnational governments, streamline procedures by disseminating standard contracts, concession agreements, and detailed procedures for identifying, evaluating, and procuring PPPs (World Bank, 2006). Standardised materials can help governments avoid problems with contract design, ensure the contracts fulfil standard requirements, and protect the public interest (Istrate and Puentes, 2011). Higher levels of government can opt for advisory rather than mandatory guidance in order to minimise the risk that standardisation constrains flexibility and innovation at the subnational level (World Bank, 2006). A PPP unit, like Partnerships Victoria (Australia), can support the procuring agency with technical demands (i.e. preparing a public sector comparator), assist with risk mitigation, help with dispute resolution, and support contract management (OECD, 2010).

What characterises effective PPP units?

Existing literature provides little guidance regarding what makes PPP units effective with respect to subnational capacity specifically, but some lessons do emerge from case study research regarding characteristics of effective PPP units generally (World Bank, 2006; 2007).

First, PPP units do not guarantee successful PPP programmes. On the one hand, often countries and subnational governments with PPP units have more robust PPP programmes than those without. In Canada, for example, the majority of transportation PPPs are concentrated in the provinces of British Columbia and Ontario, early adopters of PPP units (Lammam et al., 2013). In Germany, North-Rhine Westphalia (NRW) was the first Land to establish a PPP unit in 2001 (OECD, 2010) and it continues to lead in terms of construction PPPs at the regional and local levels (in terms of volume and value of deals since 2002) (Partnerschaften Deutschland, 2014). Yet, on the other hand, PPP units also exist in many countries without robust PPP programmes, or have multiple units with mixed results. India, for example, has multiple state-level PPP units with "different track records in terms of taking PPPs successfully to the market" (World Bank, 2006).

Second, countries with poorly performing institutions may have a poorly performing PPP unit, handicapped by the same underlying problems that undermine existing institutional performance (World Bank, 2007). Institutional reforms may need to precede or coincide with the creation of a PPP unit for it to be successful. In general, research suggests that PPP units are more likely to be effective where there is: 1) political support for the PPP programme the unit will support; 2) transparent, competitive procurement systems; and 3) generally co-ordinated machinery of government (World Bank, 2007).

Third, there is no "one size fits all" PPP unit (World Bank, 2007; Istrate and Puentes, 2011). Units tend to perform better when their authority matches their mandate, and their mandate targets the weaknesses in existing capacity to develop and implement a PPP programme (World Bank, 2007). This suggests the importance of thoughtful assessment of what factors pose the greatest constraints on subnational capacity for PPPs, evaluating which constraints are best addressed by reform, and which can be addressed through a PPP unit - and tailoring the design of and/or services offered by a unit accordingly. With respect to design, the World Bank study (2007) suggests a lack of formal authority to compel agencies to use a unit's services or comply with good practice guidance (e.g. a "center of excellence" with no authority) can render a PPP unit relatively ineffective.

Finally, backstopping and cultivating subnational capacity means that PPP units must be adequately staffed. Information made available by the World Bank (2007) suggest that the more successful PPP units appear to rely mostly on staff (e.g. Korea's PIMAC, Partnerships Victoria, Portugal's Parpublica) with some recourse to consultants. Staff stability is important for maintaining capacity and continuity. High turnover, such as observed in the past at the PPP Centre in the Philippines, can weaken effectiveness (EIU, 2012).

Importantly, PPP units are neither a panacea for subnational capacity nor are they risk-free. Conflicts of interest can arise if PPP units aim to increase deal flow and also contribute to project screening. There may be distorted incentives to seek out and approve PPPs. The potential for difficulty may be higher when the units are structured as public-private joint ventures and where "success fees incentivise the closing of transactions." (World Bank, 2006: 8). Likewise, when PPP units act as a gatekeeper, allowing only certain projects to move forward at various stages of the procurement process, regulatory controls, transparency, and accountability measures are important "to ensure honest practices and protect government interests and limit exposure to liability" (Colverson and Perera, 2012). Finally, the mere creation of a PPP unit can bias actors toward PPPs over other procurement methods (Colverson and Perera, 2012). Ensuring robust analysis of individual projects is important to counter any such bias.

Sources: OECD (2010), Dedicated Public-Private Partnership Units: A Survey of Institutional and Governance Structures, OECD Publishing, http://dx.doi.org/10.1787/9789264064843-en; Istrate, E. and R. Puentes (2011), "Moving Forward on Public Private Partnerships: US and International Experience with PPP Units", Brookings-Rockefeller Project on State and Metropolitan Innovation, Dec 2011; Colverson, S. and O. Perera (2012), "Harnessing the Power of Public-Private Partnerships: The role of hybrid financing strategies in sustainable development", International Institute for Sustainable Development, February; EIU (2012), "Evaluating the environment for public-private partnerships in Asia-Pacific: The 2011 Infrascope", Findings and methodology,

Economist Intelligence Unit; World Bank (2007), *Public-Private Partnership Units: Lessons for their Design and Use in Infrastructure*, October 2007; Dutz, M., Dhingra, I., Harris, C., and C. Shugart (2006), "Public Private Partnership Units", Public Policy for the Private Sector, Note 311, September; World Bank (2006), "India: Building capacities for public private partnerships", Sector Report No. 36875, June; Partnerschaften Deutschland (2014), "Überblickzu ÖPP-Projektenim Hoch- und Tiefbau in Deutschland", Berlin, 28 February; Lammam, C., MacIntyre, H. and J. Berechman (2013), "Using Public-Private Partnerships to Improve Transportation Infrastructure in Canada", Fraser Institute, May.

PPP units can promulgate or be accompanied by other measures to strengthen the environment in which PPPs operate. Verhoest et al. (2015) include the availability of 1) procedures appraising and prioritising projects, and 2) standardised contracts and a standardised model for PPPs.[25] The former category includes existence of standard *ex ante* evaluation instruments, use of standard *ex ante* evaluation in PPP projects, third party scrutiny and approval of PPP projects prior to tender, and third party scrutiny and approval prior to contract signature. Standardised contracts are a key feature of the UK's experience with PFI projects. To these measures, one could add other tools with potentially positive impacts for PPPs:

- **Professionalising public procurement** can strengthen capacity to undertake procurement generally, and potentially reinforce proper treatment of PPPs. As of 2010, 19 of 31 OECD countries recognised procurement officials as a specific profession (OECD, 2013a). Eleven countries have a formal job description for procurement officials, eight have implemented specific certification or licensing programmes, and five have integrity guidelines (e.g. Codes of conduct) for procurement officials (OECD, 2013a). The degree to which these mechanisms extend to and affect hiring at subnational levels of government is not clear;

- **Performance indicator systems** can strengthen PPP design and implementation by revealing information throughout the investment cycle. Performance indicators for PPPs can be adopted at both the national and subnational levels, thereby narrowing information gaps among levels of government (OECD, 2009b) and between public and private partners. Made publicly available, they strengthen transparency and accountability[26];

- **Peer-to-peer knowledge exchange platforms for subnational governments** can be used to share good practices and to benchmark local experience in a range of areas, including PPPs. In its review of PPPs, the special Panel on Public-Private Partnerships of the Transportation Committee in the US House of Representatives "encourage[s] states interested in enacting P3 authorising legislation and pursuing P3 procurements to coordinate with other states to share lessons learned by early adopters and consider establishing stand-alone state P3 offices that look beyond only transportation and develop regional partnerships to achieve common infrastructure objectives" (US HR, 2014: 13);

- **Mechanisms for inter-municipal and regional co-ordination** can be used to examine potential synergies arising from co-ordination of public investment and PPPs specifically. Provisions can be made for bundling across sectors (UNECE, 2008; Plummer, 2002) or jurisdictions to encourage economies of scale or attract operators, as well as horizontal unbundling to encourage competition and benchmarking (e.g. dividing a large area, such a city, into zones and arranging contracts for each area, Plummer, 2002); and

- **Assistance targeted to subnational PPP capacity** can help boost the design and results of these partnerships. The United Kingdom, for example, saw the creation of the "Public Private Partnership Programme" (4ps) in the mid-1990s to support PPP development at the local level in England and Wales (see the UK case study). It subsequently evolved into Local Partnerships, a joint venture between the Local Government Association and HM Treasury, which continues to support local authorities. In addition to within-country support, some subnational governments may be eligible for assistance from supra-national organisations (e.g. the Public-Private Infrastructure Advisory Facility's Subnational Technical Assistance program)[27].

Financial support and budgetary arrangements

Previous discussion has underscored the budgetary constraints that can spur consideration of PPPs, as well as the challenges and risks associated with the ordinary and contingent liabilities PPPs create. Some of the tools already discussed can play a positive role in this area. They include the existence and use of standard *ex ante* evaluation instruments, as well as third party scrutiny and approval prior to tender and/or before contract signature (which can reduce the risk of a pro-PPP bias). To these tools, other good practices can reinforce financial arrangements for PPPs. They include, for example, review by the Central Budget Authority to "ensure that the project is affordable and the overall investment envelope is sustainable" and disclosure of "all costs and contingent liabilities" in budget documentation (OECD, 2012). In 2011 the United Kingdom introduced its Whole of Government Accounts, full accruals based accounts covering the public sector that categorise PPPs largely on balance sheet, thereby minimising the accounting incentive to opt for PPPs (see the UK case study).

Direct financial support can also enhance subnational governments' ability pay for project development costs or to help cover their financial contribution to PPPs. In some cases, this support is available through PPP units. India's Gujarat Infrastructure Development Board, South Africa's PPP Center, the Philippines BOT Center (now the PPP Center), and the former Partnerships UK all provide(d) financial support for consultants working with line ministries or local governments (Dutz et al., 2006). Previously, the P3 Canada Fund covered up to 25% of eligible costs for subnational PPP infrastructure projects, including direct costs and project development costs (PPP Canada, n.d.). More recently, the Canadian government replaced the P3 Fund with the newly established Canada Infrastructure Bank (CIB), which focuses on revenue-generating infrastructure projects and leveraging private investment (Department of Finance Canada, 2016). Other institutions, such as the US Economic Development Administration, consider PPP as a competitive determinant when they provide financial support to subnational governments for infrastructure projects, in order to leverage private participation and promote regional development. As noted earlier and also discussed in Chapter 3, the United Kingdom offered financial support for subnational governments' unitary charge payments in the form of "PFI credits". As that experience revealed, it is important to evaluate the use of such support carefully to ensure that it does not distort consideration of PPPs compared to other forms of procurement.

The effectiveness of support mechanisms

Do these different supports for PPPs affect the uptake and quality of PPPs as a tool for infrastructure delivery? Are they useful for subnational governments? The three case studies that form part of this report suggest that the tools highlighted here can be useful for subnational governments. Comprehensive governance arrangements in the United Kingdom and in Virginia, at the national and subnational levels, appear to have played key roles in facilitating the uptake of PPP approaches to meet infrastructure needs. For example, the flexible and inclusive statutory framework that supports private-sector participation, along with accountability, and transparency emerges as a key contributor to the success of Virginia's PPP programme. The introduction of PPP units in both the United Kingdom and Virginia facilitated implementation of good practices and standardised procedures. Dedicated support for subnational capacity – such as Local Partnerships in England – bolstered subnational capacity, even for contract renegotiation. In addition, the shift to Whole of Government Accounts in the United Kingdom has minimised accounting incentives to move projects "off budget." That said, some mechanisms, often coming from a higher level of government, such as subsidies for availability payments, statistical or accounting treatment of PPPs, or even the presence of a PPP unit, may have the effect of unduly incentivising use of PPPs where other forms of procurement should be considered. The case study of France suggests a need for dedicated attention to administrative capacity at the subnational level to counter balance the inevitable challenges that emerge with the use of PPPs.

Conclusions

Public-private partnerships can play an important role in the toolkit of government officials. Well-designed PPPs hold potential to offer greater value for money in infrastructure investment than traditional procurement. Often, academic and practitioner literature examines PPPs through a national lens. Despite the important role of subnational governments in public investment and the place-based aspects of infrastructure, the specificities of PPPs for economic and social infrastructure at the subnational level have received limited attention.

This chapter offers a framework for examining the challenges of implementing PPPs in a decentralised context. It suggests the multi-level governance context poses important challenges in key areas such as financing and funding, intergovernmental regulatory coherence, and cross-jurisdictional co-ordination and economies of scale. The complexities of PPPs and the skills required to undertake them raise questions regarding subnational administrative capacity and accountability. These issues echo the challenges of implementing public policy in a multi-level governance context. In this case, they affect the incentives of public and private actors to engage in partnerships, the capacity of the public sector to implement them, and the quality of the PPPs they undertake.

How might governments support subnational implementation of public-private partnerships? Practitioner literature on the "good governance" of public-private partnerships maps out a multi-dimensional approach to tackling the wide range of necessary conditions for effective PPPs. Recommendations cover areas such as political and policy commitment, legal and regulatory frameworks, institutional arrangements, administrative tools, budgetary arrangements, and financial support. Again, with some exceptions, the focus is largely national. This chapter has considered how such mechanisms can and currently do play out at the subnational level. It suggests that both multi-dimensional and multi-level governance considerations are important for subnational PPPs.

Notes

1. Which functions are transferred to the private sector generally determines the type of PPP.
2. See, for example, the brief discussion of PPPs in OECD (2013c) for summary of the main advantage of and some difficulties associated with PPPs.
3. "A PPP project is affordable if the expenditure it implies for the government can be accommodated with current levels of government expenditure and revenue and if it can be assumed that such levels will be and can be sustained into the future" OECD (2008: 39).
4. "Value for money" is an assessment of the "optimal combination of quality, features and price, calculated over the whole of the project's life" (OECD, 2008: 21). For a brief discussion of the limits to value for money assessment, see Public Works Financing (2014).
5. Data come from the World Bank Private Participation in Infrastructure database, which tracks private participation in middle- and low-income countries in four key sectors: energy, ICT, water, and transport. It includes four categories of projects: management and lease contracts, brownfield projects, Greenfield projects, and divestitures. Private participation must be at least 20% of the contract, except for divestitures where the threshold is at least 5% of equity owned by private parties. (World Bank, 2016b).
6. This figure combines PPPs that Park (2013: 26) categorises as "central+local government" (161 local government projects with a significant central subsidy) and "local government" projects (307 projects for which provinces or cities are the competent authority). The total number of projects at all levels of government is 633.
7. The case study describes the methodology for assigning projects to different levels of government based on the procuring authority. Data used in the analysis come from HM Treasury (2014a).
8. Just as they may contribute to or detract from public investment at the subnational level, see OECD (2013c).
9. For a discussion of rural infrastructure in the US and EU contexts, see for example Blandford et al. (2008).
10. Hooghe and Marks (2003, 2010) describe two categories of multi-level governance. Type I governance is associated with the dispersion of authority to a "limited number of multitask, general-purpose jurisdictions with nonintersecting borders" (Hooghe and Marks, 2003) such as local, regional, national (and supra-national) governments. By contrast, Type II governance "operate[s] at numerous territorial scales... jurisdictions are task-specific rather than general-purpose ... and flexible rather than durable" (Hooghe and Marks, 2010). In this case the unit of analysis is the functional jurisdiction, created to respond to a particular policy problem and at the correspondingly appropriate scale. PPPs for infrastructure and service provision straddle both Type I and Type II: they are often legally created, regulated, and financed in Type I systems but address functional issues that may cross jurisdictions and operate in an environment with Type II stakeholders.

11. Now PF2.
12. In 2013, of 80 PPP deals reaching financial close in Europe, 14 transactions benefitted from some form of public financing and/or guarantee commitment (EPEC, 2014).
13. This discussion and example of the challenges of financing small PPPs come from S. Shukla (personal communication, May 6, 2014).
14. Private actors must consider the full weight of taxes to which a PPP will be subject. Such taxes may occur at multiple levels of government (UNCITRAL, 2001).
15. In Argentina, for example, a sometimes-difficult relationship between the national government and provincial ones, along with increasing provincial dependence on intergovernmental transfers has made provinces vulnerable to changes in national funding decisions, increasing risk for the private sector (EIU, 2013b).
16. They recommend a gradual increase in prices, starting before the public authorities have transitioned to private participation (Beato and Vives, 2003). The authors are referring to private participation in infrastructure generally and not PPPs specifically.
17. See also Beato and Vives (2003) and Harper and Daughters (2007) for discussion of regulatory issues.
18. These include "licences under foreign exchange regulations; licences for the incorporation of the concessionaire; authorisations for the employment of foreigners; registration and stamp duties for the use or ownership of land; import licences for equipment and supplies; construction licences; licences for the installation of cables or pipelines; licences for bringing the facility into operation; and spectrum allocation for mobile communication" (UNCITRAL, 2001: 30).
19. See also Plummer (2002: 263).
20. According to the Latin America Infrascope Model 2012 (EIU, 2013b), "Brazil's legal mechanisms for establishing PPP projects are effective at different layers of government. The federal government has exclusive rights to grant PPP projects in the energy sector and with respect to interstate roads, railroads, airports and seaports. State and municipal governments are responsible for water distribution, sewage and metropolitan, urban and state road projects." It further found, "Individual state frameworks cannot contradict or override federal legislation" but "the institutional framework varies for each state, creating a heterogeneous environment for state-level projects."
21. S. Shukla, personal communication, May 6, 2014.
22. The advisory market may not always be as well developed as subnational governments may need, however. The experience of the Netherlands is instructive here. According to Koster (2005), early experiences with PPPs needed to tap both Dutch and UK advisors due to lack of experience and limited sophistication in the Dutch advisory market. This raised costs and led to a less-than-efficient structuring of early contracts based on the UK's common law system rather than a Dutch model.
23. The quote is from the Latin America Infrascope Model 2012, country detail for Mexico in Excel (EIU, 2013b).
24. The authors use the framework as the basis of a PPP Government Support Index (PPP GSI).

25. As Verhoest et al. (2015) base their research on analysis of transportation PPPs, the model contract they propose would be for transportation PPPs, but one could argue that such a tool could be applied more generally to other sectors.
26. For a discussion of data and PPPs see, for example, World Bank (2016d).
27. The Public-Private Infrastructure Advisory Facility (PPIAF) is a multi-donor technical assistance facility to help developing countries tap the potential of private sector involvement in infrastructure. It features a Subnational Technical Assistance programme that works to enhance SNGs' access to market-based financing without sovereign guarantees (PPIAF, 2014).

References

Beato, P. and A. Vives (2003), "Private Infrastructure Investment at the Subnational Level: Challenges in Emerging Economies", *IADB Working Paper*, Inter-American Development Bank, Washington, DC, October, https://pdfs.semanticscholar.org/52ec/f59652b683ff48010cf8cfe182adf7e49df4.pdf.

Blandford, D., R.N. Boisvert and S. Davidova (2008), "Infrastructure and Rural Development: US and EU Perspectives", *EuroChoices*, 7(1), pp. 52-59, http://dx.doi.org/10.1111/j.1746-692X.2008.00086.x.

Brookings Institution (2012), "Brookings Calls on Obama Administration to Establish a Federal PPP Unit to Support Infrastructure Investment", The Metropolitan Policy Program at Brookings, Press Release, 13 November, wwww.brookings.edu/wp-content/uploads/2016/06/13-public-private-infrastructure-release.pdf.

Burger, P. and I. Hawkesworth (2011), "How to Attain Value for Money: Comparing PPP and Traditional Infrastructure Public Procurement", *OECD Journal on Budgeting*, Volume 11/1, pp. 91–146, http://dx.doi.org/10.1787/budget-11-5kg9zc0pvq6j.

Canadian Council for Public-Private Partnerships (2011), "Public-Private Partnerships: A Guide for Municipalities", with PPP Canada, November, www.pppcouncil.ca/web/P3_Knowledge_Centre/Research/Public-Private_Partnerships___A_Guide_for_Municipalities__.aspx.

Canadian Council for Public-Private Partnerships (n.d.), *Project Database*, http://projects.pppcouncil.ca/ (accessed 1 May 2017).

Charbit, C. and M. Michalun (2009), "Mind the gaps: Managing mutual dependence in relations among levels of government", *OECD Working Papers on Public Governance*, No. 14, OECD Publishing, Paris, http://dx.doi.org/10.1787/221253707200.

Colverson, S. and O. Perera (2012), *Harnessing the Power of Public-Private Partnerships: The Role of Hybrid Financing Strategies in Sustainable Development*, International Institute for Sustainable Development, Winnipeg and Geneva, February, www.iisd.org/publications/pub.aspx?id=1550.

Dutz, M., I. Dhingra, C. Harris and C. Shugart (2006), "Public Private Partnership Units: What Are They, and What Do They Do?", *Viewpoint: Public Policy for the Private Sector*, Note No. 311, World Bank, Washington, DC, http://hdl.handle.net/10986/11175.

EC (European Commission) (2014a), "Memo, Directive of the European Parliament and of the Council on the award of Concession Contracts – Frequently Asked Questions", 15 January 2014 http://europa.eu/rapid/press-release_MEMO-14-19_fr.htm (accessed 27 April 2015).

EC (2014b), "New Rules on Public Contracts and Concessions: Simpler and More Flexible", Leaflet, Internal Market and Services, European Union, Luxembourg, http://dx.doi.org/10.2780/45535.

EIU (Economist Intelligence Unit) (2013a), "Evaluating the environment for public-private partnerships in Latin America and the Caribbean: The 2012 Infrascope", Index guide and methodology, The Economist Intelligence Unit, London, http://infrascope.eiu.com/wp-content/uploads/2017/02/Latin-America_Infrascope_Report_2012_English.pdf.

EIU (2013b), "Latin America Infrascope Model 2012", Excel workbook, The Economist Intelligence Unit, London, http://infrascope.eiu.com/wp-content/uploads/2017/02/Latin-America_Infrascope_Model_2012.xls.

EIU (2013c), "Evaluating the environment for public-private partnerships in Eastern Europe and the Commonwealth of Independent States: The 2012 EECIS Infrascope", Findings and methodology, The Economist Intelligence Unit, London, http://infrascope.eiu.com/wp-content/uploads/2017/02/Europe_Infrascope_Report_2012_English.pdf.

EIU (2012), "Evaluating the environment for public-private partnerships in Asia-Pacific: The 2011 Infrascope", Findings and methodology, The Economist Intelligence Unit and the Asian Development Bank, London and Manila, http://infrascope.eiu.com/wp-content/uploads/2017/02/Asia-Pacific_Infrascope_Report_2011_English.pdf.

EPEC (European PPP Expertise Centre) (2014), "Market Update: Review of the European PPP Market in 2013", European PPP Expertise Centre, Brussels, February, www.eib.org/attachments/epec/epec_market_update_2013_en.pdf.

EPEC (2012a), "France PPP Units and Related Institutional Framework", European PPP Expertise Centre, Brussels, May, www.eib.org/infocentre/publications/all/epec-france-ppp-unit-and-related-institutional-framework.htm.

EPEC (2012b), "Project Finance" in "The Guide to Guidance: How to Prepare, Procure and Deliver PPP Projects", www.eib.org/epec/g2g/annex/1-project-finance (accessed 22 January 2014).

EPEC (2011), "State Guarantees in PPPs: A Guide to Better Evaluation, Design, Implementation and Management", European PPP Expertise Centre, Brussels, May, www.minfin.bg/upload/13582/epec-state-guarantees-in-ppps-public.pdf.

Farlex Financial Dictionary (2012), "Take-Out Commitment", webpage, http://financial-dictionary.thefreedictionary.com/Take+Out+Financing (accessed 9 December 2013).

Farrugia, C., T. Reynolds and R. Orr (2008), "Public-Private Partnership Agencies: A Global Perspective", *Working Paper* 39, Collaboratory for Research on Global Projects, Stanford University, August, https://gpc.stanford.edu/sites/default/files/wp039_0.pdf.

Gifford, J. and M. Transue (2018), "Public-private partnerships for infrastructure at the sub-national level of government: Opportunities and challenges in the Commonwealth of Virginia", Chapter 4 of this report.

Harper, L. and R. Daughters (2007), "Public-private partnerships: Trends and challenges at the subnational level", conference paper, XII Congreso Internacional del CLAD sobre la Reforma del Estado y de la Administración Pública, Sto. Domingo, Rep. Dominicana, 30 Oct - 2 Nov 2007, www.clad.org/siare_isis/fulltext/0057912.pdf.

HM Treasury (2014a), "Current projects as at 31 March 2014", Excel workbook, www.gov.uk/government/uploads/system/uploads/attachment_data/file/387225/current_projects_as_at_31_March_2014.xlsx.

HM Treasury (2014b), "Private Finance Initiative projects: 2014 summary data", December 2014, www.gov.uk/government/uploads/system/uploads/attachment_data/file/387228/pfi_projects_2014_summary_data_final_15122014.pdf.

HM Treasury (2012), "A new approach to public private partnerships", December, www.gov.uk/government/uploads/system/uploads/attachment_data/file/205112/pf2_infrastructure_new_approach_to_public_private_parnerships_051212.pdf.

Hooghe, L. and G. Marks (2010), "Types of Multilevel Governance", in Enderlein, H., S. Wälti and M. Zürn (eds.), *Handbook on Multilevel Governance*, Edward Elgar, Cheltenham.

Hooghe, L. and G. Marks (2003), "Unraveling the Central State, but How? Types of Multi-level Governance", *American Political Science Review,* 97(02), pp. 233-243, http://dx.doi.org/10.1017/S0003055403000649.

Infrastructure Australia (2014), "Public Private Partnerships", webpage, http://infrastructureaustralia.gov.au/policy-publications/public-private-partnerships/index.aspx (accessed 22 March 2018).

Infrastructure Australia (2008), "National PPP Guidelines: Policy Framework", December.

Infrastructure Concession Regulatory Commission (2012), "6.4 Sources of Finance" in "PPP Manual for Nigeria", ICRC.

International Monetary Fund (2014), World Economic Outlook, October 2014.

Istrate, E. and R. Puentes (2011), "Moving Forward on Public Private Partnerships: US and International Experience with PPP Units", Brookings-Rockefeller Project on State and Metropolitan Innovation, Brookings Institution, Washington, DC, December, wwwwww.brookings.edu/wp-content/uploads/2016/06/1208_transportation_istrate_puentes.pdf.

Jooste, S., and R.E. Levitt (2009), "The impacts of infrastructure PPPs on Public Sector Capacity", Proceedings of the ASCE Construction Research Congress, Seattle, WA, 5-7 April 2009, https://gpc.stanford.edu/sites/default/files/cp031_0.pdf.

Kappeler, A., A. Solé-Ollé, A. Stephan and T. Välilä (2012), "Does Fiscal Decentralization Foster Regional Investment in Productive Infrastructure?", *DIW Berlin Discussion Paper*, No. 1204, DeutschesInstitutfürWirtschaftsforschung, Berlin, http://dx.doi.org/10.2139/ssrn.2050355.

Koster, J. (2005), "Public-private partnerships: Netherlands switches on to public-private deals", *International Financial Law Review*, 23 May, www.iflr.com/Article/1984888/Public-private-partnerships-Netherlands-switches-on-to-public-private-deals.html (accessed 28 April 2015).

Lammam, C., H. MacIntyre and J. Berechman (2013), "Using Public-Private Partnerships to Improve Transportation Infrastructure in Canada", *Studies in Economic Prosperity*, Fraser Institute, May, www.fraserinstitute.org/sites/default/files/using-public-private-partnerships-to-improve-transportation-infrastructure-in-canada-rev.pdf.

Mathieson, S.A. (2014), "Scotland's prescription for health: Ditch the PFI", *The Guardian*, 22 January 2014, www.theguardian.com/society/2014/jan/22/scotland-health-ditch-pfi-nhs (accessed 12 February 2014).

McKinsey & Co. (2016), "Bridging Global Infrastructure Gaps", McKinsey Global Institute, Capital Projects and Infrastructure Practice, June, www.mckinsey.com/industries/capital-projects-and-infrastructure/our-insights/bridging-global-infrastructure-gaps (accessed 10 May 2017).

Mizell, L. (2018), "Public-private partnerships at the sub-national level of government: The case of PFI in the United Kingdom", Chapter 3 of this report.

Mizell, L. and D. Allain-Dupré (2013), "Creating conditions for effective public investment: Sub-national capacities in a multi-level governance context*", OECD Regional Development Working Papers*, No. 2013/04, OECD Publishing, Paris, http://dx.doi.org/10.1787/5k49j2cjv5mq-en.

Moszoro, M. and P. Gąsiorowski (2008), "Optimal capital structure of public-private partnerships", *IMF Working Papers*, WP/08/1, January, www.imf.org/external/pubs/ft/wp/2008/wp0801.pdf.

Musson, S. (2009), "The Geography of the Private Finance Initiative", *Geographical Paper* 188, University of Reading, www.reading.ac.uk/web/FILES/geographyandenvironmentalscience/GP188.pdf.

OECD (2017) Investing in Climate, Investing in Growth, OECD Publishing, Paris, http://dx.doi.org/10.1787/9789264273528-en.

OECD (2016), *OECD Regions at a Glance 2016*, OECD Publishing, Paris, http://dx.doi.org/10.1787/reg_glance-2016-en.

OECD (2014), "Recommendation of the Council on Effective Public Investment Across Levels of Government", 12 March, wwww.oecd.org/regional/regional-policy/Principles-Public-Investment.pdf.

OECD (2013a), *Government at a Glance 2013*, OECD Publishing, Paris, http://dx.doi.org/10.1787/gov_glance-2013-en.

OECD (2013b), *Fiscal Federalism 2014: Making Decentralisation Work*, OECD Publishing, Paris, http://dx.doi.org/10.1787/9789264204577-en.

OECD (2013c), "Investing for Inclusive Growth: Principles for Action" in *Regions and Cities: Where Policies and People Meet*, Policy Briefs prepared for the 3rd Ministerial Meeting of the Territorial Development Policy Committee, Marseille, France, 5-6 December, pg. 5, www.oecd.org/regional/ministerial/policy-briefs.pdf.

OECD (2012), "Recommendation of the Council on Principles for Public Governance of Public-Private Partnerships", May, www.oecd.org/governance/budgeting/PPP-Recommendation.pdf.

OECD (2010), *Dedicated Public-Private Partnership Units: A Survey of Institutional and Governance Structures*, OECD Publishing, Paris, http://dx.doi.org/10.1787/9789264064843-en.

OECD (2009a), "Bridging the Gaps between Levels of Government", OECD Policy Brief, October.

OECD (2009b), *Governing Regional Development Policy: The Use of Performance Indicators*, OECD Publishing, Paris, http://dx.doi.org/10.1787/9789264056299-en.

OECD (2008), *Public-Private Partnerships: In Pursuit of Risk Sharing and Value for Money*, OECD Publishing, Paris, http://dx.doi.org/10.1787/9789264046733-en.

OECD (2007), "Executive summary", in *Globalisation and Regional Economies: Can OECD Regions Compete in Global Industries?*, OECD Publishing, Paris, http://dx.doi.org/10.1787/9789264037809-2-en.

Park, H. (2013), "PPP (Public-Private Partnerships) System in Korea", presentation, 21 November, www.kdevelopedia.org/mnt/idas/asset/2013/11/29/DOC/PDF/04201311290129319073742.pdf.

Partnerschaften Deutschland (2014), "Überblickzu ÖPP-Projektenim Hoch- und Tiefbau in Deutschland", Berlin, 28 February, www.partnerschaften-deutschland.de/fileadmin/Daten/OEPP-Markt/OEPP-Marktzahlen/140303_Projektdatenbank_PPP-Projekte_Dt__Stand_Ende_Februar2014.pdf.

Partnerships Bulletin (2012), "The Global PPP Market2012", with PPP Bulletin and Deloitte, www2.deloitte.com/content/dam/Deloitte/global/Documents/gx-icp-the-global-ppp-market-2012.pdf.

Petersen, O.H. (2011), "Multi-level governance of public-private partnerships: An analysis of the Irish case", *Handuskuluur – Administrative Culture* 12 (2), 162-188, http://halduskultuur.eu/journal/index.php/HKAC/article/download/57/53.

Plummer, J. (2002), *Focusing Partnerships a Sourcebook for Municipal Capacity Building in Public-Private Partnerships,* Earthscan, London and Sterling, www.undp.org/content/dam/aplaws/publication/en/publications/capacity-development/municipal-capacity-building-in-public-private-partnerships/Municipal-Capacity-Building.pdf.

PPIAF (Public-Private Infrastructure Advisory Facility) (2014), "About Us" and "Sub-National Technical Assistance Program", webpages, https://ppiaf.org/about-us and https://ppiaf.org/sub-national-ta (accessed 18 September 2017).

PPIAF and PWC (PriceWaterhouseCoopers) (2006), "Hybrid PPPs: Levering EU Funds and Private Capital", January, www.irfnet.ch/files-upload/knowledges/PWC_HybridPPPs_2006.pdf.

PPP Canada (n.d.), "Application Guide and Application Form Round Seven, April 13, 2015 – June 12, 2015".

Public Works Financing (2014), *Public Works Financing*, P3 Research Issue, January, www.pwfinance.net/document/P3_Research_Issue.pdf.

Public Works Financing (2013), "World P3 Market by Sector/Country (10/13)", The International Major Projects database 2013, http://pwfinance.net/research/reprints/ and www.pwfinance.net/document/research_reprints/Charts%201013/Big%20chart.pdf.

PWC (PriceWaterhouseCoopers) (2013), "Overview of global PPP markets", OECD 2013 annual meeting of senior PPP officials, 15 April, www.oecd.org/gov/budgeting/D1-AM%20-%20S1%20-%20Charles%20LLOYD%20-%20PWC.pdf.

Rall, J., J. Reed and N. Farber (2010), "Public-Private Partnerships for Transportation: A Toolkit for Legislators", National Conference of State Legislatures, Denver and Washington, DC, October, www.ncsl.org/documents/transportation/ppptoolkit.pdf.

Richardson, L. (2010), "The Value of a Proper Enabling Environment for PPP's in Infrastructure Investment and Development", Institute for Public-Private Partnerships, Public-Private Partnership Information Series, February.

Saragiotis, P. (ed.) (2009), "Public-Private Partnerships in Infrastructure Days 2008", proceedings of the conference held 15-18 December 2008, World Bank Institute, Washington, DC, http://documents.worldbank.org/curated/en/301771468337169167/Public-private-partnerships-in-infrastructure-days-2008.

Saussier, S. (2017), "Public-private partnerships for infrastructure at the sub-national level of government: Opportunities and challenges in France", Chapter 2 of this report.

Sénat (2014), "Les Contrats de Partenariat: Des Bombes à Retardement?", Synthesis note of the report by Mr. Hugues Portelli and Mr. Jean-Pierre Sueur, July, www.senat.fr/notice-rapport/2013/r13-733-notice.html (accessed 23 March 2018).

Shenk, S. (2015a), "I-95 Tolls Bring in $9 Million in First Quarter", Fredericksburg.com, 25 April, www.fredericksburg.com/news/transportation/i--tolls-bring-in-million-in-first-quarter/article_c198630e-fe30-5d82-be37-9fe4e0929232.html, as cited in Gifford, J. and M. Transue (2018), "Public-private partnerships for infrastructure at the sub-national level of government: Opportunities and challenges in the Commonwealth of Virginia", Chapter 4 of this report.

Shenk, S. (2015b), "I-95 Express Lanes Continue to Rake in the Money, Ringing up $15 Million in the Second Quarter", Fredericksburg.com, 11 July, wwww.fredericksburg.com/news/transportation/i--express-lanes-continue-to-rake-in-the-money/article_4913b520-593e-533e-8bb4-f1198c2ae7f5.html, as cited in Gifford, J. and M. Transue (2018), "Public-private partnerships for infrastructure at the subnational level of government: Opportunities and challenges in the Commonwealth of Virginia", Chapter 4 of this report.

UNCITRAL (United Nations Commission on International Trade Law) (2001), "Legislative Guide on Privately Financed Infrastructure Projects", United Nations, New York, www.uncitral.org/pdf/english/texts/procurem/pfip/guide/pfip-e.pdf .

UNECE (United Nations Economic Commission for Europe) (2008), *Guidebook on Promoting Good Governance in Public-Private Partnerships*, United Nations, New York and Geneva, January, www.unece.org/fileadmin/DAM/ceci/publications/ppp.pdf.

US HR (United States House of Representatives Committee on Transportation and Infrastructure) (2014), "Public Private Partnerships: Balancing the needs of the public and private sectors to finance the nation's infrastructure", Findings of the Special Panel on Public-Private Partnerships, http://transportation.house.gov/uploadedfiles/p3_panel_report.pdf.

Verhoest, K., O.H. Petersen, W. Scherrer and R.M. Soecipto (2015), "How Do Governments Support the Development of Public–Private Partnerships? Measuring and Comparing PPP Governmental Support in 20 European Countries", *Transport Reviews: A Transnational Transdisciplinary Journal*, Vol. 35(2), pp. 118-139, http://dx.doi.org/10.1080/01441647.2014.993746.

Virginia Department of Transportation (2012), "Comprehensive Agreement Relating to the I-95 HOV/HOT Lanes Project", as cited in Gifford, J. and M. Transue (2018), "Public-private partnerships for infrastructure at the sub-national level of government: Opportunities and challenges in the Commonwealth of Virginia", Chapter 4 of this report.

Virginia Department of Transportation (2007), "Amended and Restated Comprehensive Agreement Relating to the Route 495 HOT Lanes in Virginia Project", as cited in Gifford, J. and M. Transue (2018), "Public-private partnerships for infrastructure at the sub-national level of government: Opportunities and challenges in the Commonwealth of Virginia", Chapter 4 of this report.

Von Thadden, G. (2012), "Financing Municipal PPPs", European PPP Expertise Centre, Brussels, 6 June 2012, http://ec.europa.eu/economy_finance/events/2012/2012-06-06-ec-epec/documents/epec_-_g.von_thadden.pdf.

WEF (World Economic Forum) (2013), "Strategic Infrastructure: Steps to Prepare and Accelerate Public-Private Partnerships", in collaboration with The Boston Consulting Group, World Economic Forum, Geneva, May, www3.weforum.org/docs/AF13/WEF_AF13_Strategic_Infrastructure_Initiative.pdf.

WEF (2012), "Strategic Infrastructure: Steps to Prioritize and Deliver Infrastructure Effectively and Efficiently", in collaboration with PWC, World Economic Forum, Geneva, September, www.weforum.org/reports/strategic-infrastructure-steps-prioritize-and-deliver-infrastructure-effectively-and-efficiently.

World Bank (2017), *World Development Indicators*, Online tables: 3.5 Freshwater (http://wdi.worldbank.org/table/3.5), 3.12 Urbanization (http://wdi.worldbank.org/table/3.12), 3.13 Sustainable Energy for All (http://wdi.worldbank.org/table/3.13), last updated 17 April 2017 (accessed 12 May 2017).

World Bank (2016a), *World Development Indicators 2016*, World Bank, Washington, DC, http://dx.doi.org/10.1596/978-1-4648-0683-4.

World Bank (2016b), "Methodology", *Private Participation in Infrastructure Database*, webpage, http://ppi.worldbank.org/methodology/ppi-methodology (accessed 12 May 2017).

World Bank (2016c), "Government Support in Financing PPPs", webpage, (last updated 8 September 2016) and "Risk Mitigation Mechanisms", webpage, (last updated 31 October 16), The Public-Private

Partnership in Infrastructure Resource Center (PPPIRC), http://ppp.worldbank.org/public-private-partnership/financing (accessed 12 May 2017).

World Bank (2016d), "Data", *Handshake*, April, https://handshake.pppknowledgelab.org/issues/data (accessed 2 June 2017).

World Bank (2011), "Transformation through infrastructure, Issues and Concept Note", World Bank Group Infrastructure Strategy Update, World Bank, Washington, DC.

World Bank (2007), *Public-private partnership units: Lessons for their design and use in infrastructure*, World Bank, Washington, DC, http://documents.worldbank.org/curated/en/220171468332941865/Public-private-partnership-units-lessons-for-their-design-and-use-in-infrastructure.

World Bank (2006), "India: Building Capacities for Public Private Partnerships", World Bank, Washington, DC, http://hdl.handle.net/10986/19446.

World Bank Institute and PPIAF (2012), "Public-Private Partnerships: Reference Guide Version 1.0", World Bank, Washington, DC, http://hdl.handle.net/10986/16055.

World Highways (2016), "France replaces P3 advisory body MAPPP with Fin Infra", webpage, 31 May 2016, www.worldhighways.com/categories/auctions-equipment-supply-servicing-finance/news/france-replaces-p3-advisory-body-mappp-with-fin-infra/ (accessed 11 May 2017).

Yescombe, E. (2013), *Principles of Project Finance*, 2nd Edition, Academic Press, GoogleBooks (accessed 22 January 2014).

Chapter 2. Public-private partnerships for infrastructure at the subnational level of government: Opportunities and challenges in France

by Stéphane Saussier

This chapter presents a case study of public-private partnerships (PPPs) for infrastructure development in France. The first part of this chapter presents briefly the context for PPPs in France. In the second part, the challenges associated with the development of subnational PPPs are explored by looking at the cases of the city of Caen and Paris. The last section highlights the main findings, challenges and recommendations for foming forward. In particular, it suggests the creation of a a national observatory in charge of collecting data, informing and training local public authorities not only for PPPs, but more broadly for public-private complex infrastructure contracts.

Introduction

After a short-lived expansion in reaction to the 2008 financial crisis, public investment has experienced a substantial decline in a number of European countries (OECD, 2013). As a natural reaction to these budget cuts, more efficient use of increasingly limited resources is put in the limelight: "Doing more with less" has become the mantra of this decade. Those financial constraints have been translated by a changing role of the government itself. Moving from own production to delegation and externalisation, the public sector has shifted its focus from dealing with the internal bureaucracy to managing relations with external partners through public-private partnerships (PPPs). As a result of this transition, which began before the financial crisis, the typical job description of public managers and bureaucrats has significantly changed over the last decades.

This chapter addresses difficulties related to the decision to go through public-private partnerships. In what follows, we will refer to the OECD's definition of PPPs as:

> *long-term contractual agreements between the government and a private partner whereby the latter typically finances and delivers public services using a capital asset (e.g. transport or energy infrastructure, hospital or school buildings). The private party may be tasked with the design, construction, financing, operation, management and delivery of the service for a pre-determined period of time, receiving its compensation from fixed unitary payments or tolls charged to users.* (OECD, 2008)

While these new forms of providing public services are mainly chosen as a reaction to limited resources and with the aim of accessing private sector expertise to overcome limited public sector capabilities, this shift created a set of new capacity challenges for the public sector: partial contracting out of government services requires specific types of contracting capacity (Brown and Potoski, 2003). In fact, such capacity might be a necessary condition for success and as such needs to be carefully studied. The question of administrative contracting capability as a determinant of performance has not received enough attention. In order to understand and reconcile the large variation in PPPs and contracting out performance with the theoretical predictions, it appears indispensable to put the spotlight on administrative skills. This is one of the objectives of this report. More specifically, through case studies of specific cities, we put forward several propositions in order to foster opportunities, overcome challenges and create supportive arrangements for PPPs at the subnational level in France.

The first part of this chapter presents briefly the context for PPPs in France. In the second part, the challenges associated with the development of sub-national PPPs are explored by looking at the cases of the city of Caen – a medium-sized city in France – and the city of Paris. As expected, the types of problems encountered by medium-sized and large cities are not the same. In the last section, the main results are presented. It is also highlighted that the new European public procurement and concession directives might deeply affect the rules of the game. These new directives, voted in early 2014, have been translated into national laws – the deadline to translate the Directives was April 2016. These directives, instead of pushing for more central or regional regulation, bet on a decentralised regulation based on more transparency (Saussier et Tirole, 2015). If this might be a good way to foster competition, it will not help reduce capability shortages for some cities to develop PPPs in a near future. One potential avenue to develop such capacities is to create a national observatory in charge of collecting data, informing and training local public authorities not only for PPPs, but more broadly for public-private complex infrastructure contracts.

Country context for subnational PPPs

Infrastructure needs in Europe and in France

Total public investment is a sizeable sum in France, with nearly EUR 80 billion invested in 2014. Most of public investment is done at the subnational level. In 2015, local public administration invested more than EUR 50 billion in infrastructure, accounting for more than 60% of total public investment. This illustrates that a substantial portion of public investments is made at the local level. There is a need to think carefully about the efficiency of local public investments and potential ways to foster it. This is particularly important at times, and in places, where there is a need for high-cost infrastructure investment, for example in transport, as well as to support the delivery of other public services.

Tools for investing in public infrastructure

There are three main tools available to local public authorities for investing in public infrastructure: 1) traditional public procurement; 2) concessions; and 3) availability-based contracts. For the purpose of this chapter, concession contracts and availability-based contracts will be the main focus.

Public procurement

In France, as in most of the world, traditional public procurement is the main tool used for infrastructure investment. According to the French Economic Observatory of Public Procurement of the French Ministry of Finance (OEAP), in 2013, procurement contracts accounted for around EUR 72 billion before tax in France (for some 96 500 contracts). OEAP data, however, only accounts for contracts above a threshold of EUR 90 000. With this in mind, public procurement contracts are believed to amount to about EUR 200 billion a year in France, or 10% of the gross domestic product (GDP), of which around 35% is dedicated to infrastructure.

Concession contracts

Concession contracts, a second tool for investing in infrastructure, have a long history in France, dating back to the 17th century. Through concession contracts, a public legal entity entrusts its investment needs and the management of a public service under its responsible to a public or private entity in return for a payment that depends on the results of the service operation. End users are usually (with the exception of shadow tolls) those who pay the concessionaire.

In France, such contracts are very common. They are employed for mass catering, water and sanitation, district heating, transport, sports facilities, etc. There is no concessions observatory in France (as it is the case for public procurement contracts with OEAP) to inventory ongoing concession projects. However, it is generally estimated that concessions in France generate a volume of business of over EUR 100 billion a year for operators alone (Institut de la Gestion Déléguée, 2011), or around 5% of the GDP (around half of which comes from transport initiatives).

Availability-based contracts

Launched in June 2004, "public-private partnership contracts" – very similar to private finance initiative (PFI) contracts in the United Kingdom – enable a public entity to entrust a company with a project as part of a long-term contract in return for a staggered payment from the public entity conditioned to key performance indicators (availability-based payment contract). It is used for major construction projects (educational establishments, train stations, etc.), urban infrastructure (street lighting, roads, etc.) and even sports and cultural facilities (theatres, stadiums, swimming pools, etc.).

The introduction of this new kind of PPP was primarily designed to help France catch up to other countries, such as the United Kingdom, which has used this type of tool since the early 1990s. While there have been an increasing number of availability-based contracts signed between 2005 and 2012, the total value of these contracts lags well behind the other two public procurement tools. Between 2004 and 2015 around 0.2% of the GDP and about EUR 14 billion in infrastructure investment have been financed through availability-based contracts in France. This amounts to less than 3% of public investment in infrastructure made over this period. The majority of contracts have been signed at the local level (city or urban areas). Contracts signed at the local level are of lower value (the average amount at local level is EUR 28 million compared to an average of EUR 220 million for contracts signed at the state level). According to the French PPP Task Force - Fin Infra, the EUR 3.5 billion spent at the local level over the 2004-15 period was allocated as follows:

- 41% to sport and leisure infrastructure (mainly stadiums);
- 23% to education infrastructure (mainly schools);
- 13% to lighting, car parks, and waste management;
- 11% to transportation;
- 7% to information technology; and
- 5% the renovation of buildings to achieve better energy performance.

The fact that the use of availability-based PPPs in France is largely developed but still small compared to traditional public procurement contracts should not be interpreted as the result of difficulties specific to this type of PPP. Traditional public procurement contracts are considered as the natural way to provide infrastructure, largely because of a French law of 1985, known as “the MOP law”, concerning “public contracting authorities and their relations with private contractors”. In addition, availability-based PPPs are subject to legal constraints (value- for- money reports) that do not exist yet for traditional public procurement contracts and which make them more difficult to use for a public authority.

However, distinguishing among the available tools for investing in public infrastructure is useful. First, because it highlights that PPPs refer to two different ways to finance infrastructure, namely concession and availability-based contracts. Second, because problems associated with PPPs are common to both types. However, availability-based and concession contracts also have also problems that are specific and that may explain why one form of PPPs will be preferred over the other at the subnational level.

Figure 2.1. Amount of investment in infrastructure: French availability-based contracts between 2004 and 2015 (October)

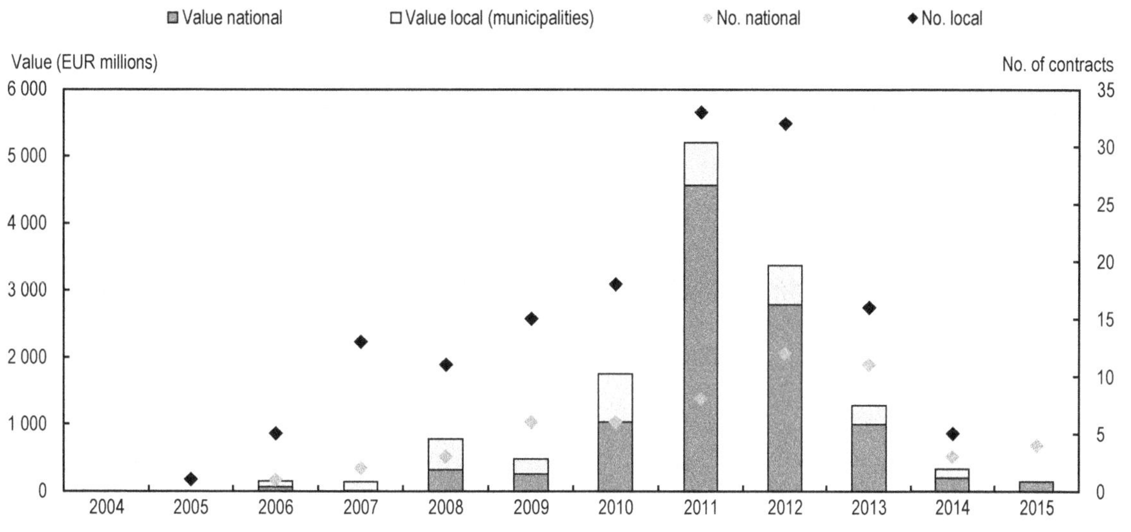

Source: Fin Infra, data updated 8 October 2015.

Figure 2.2. Type of infrastructures financed at the local level (by level of investments) (2015)

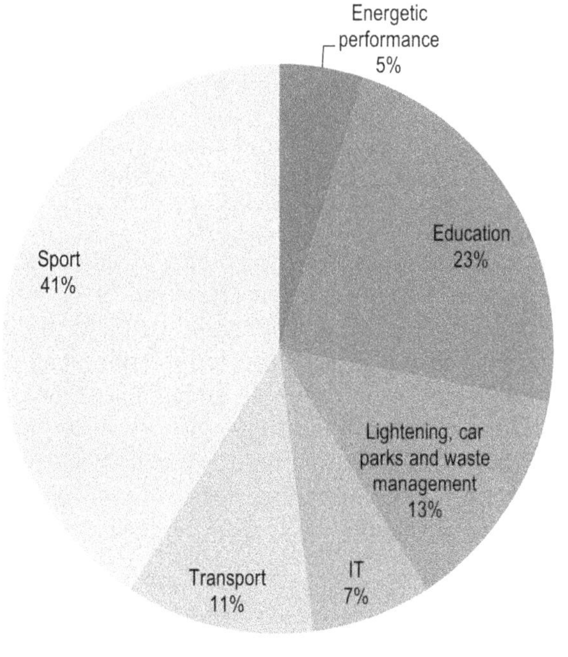

Source: Fin Infra

Challenges associated with PPPs in France

What does the theory suggest?

The economics of PPPs is now largely developed (Saussier and Tirole, 2015). Williamson (1976) highlights several fundamental problems associated with public-private partnerships: organising competition for the market is not easy; transaction costs make contracts necessarily incomplete; and switching costs make public authorities who enter contracts vulnerable to *ex post* contractual opportunism.

One problem local public authorities face is organising a competitive market in order to select the most efficient partner to provide a service (Chong, Huet and Saussier, 2006). This is challenging because the selection process itself may be complex, requiring the specification of a vector of prices for different types of customers, consuming at different times, and for different levels of quality. Moreover, if operators are selected according to price bids, then public authorities are vulnerable to the "winner's curse", since the best offer may come from the most "optimistic" operator who unintentionally underestimates production costs or overestimates future revenues. This problem is especially true for concession contracts but not for availability-based contracts because revenues for these do not come from future demand.

Alternatively, public authorities may also need to manage aggressive bidding situations. These arise when prospective operators strategically underestimate production costs or overestimate future revenues in order to win the deal and then provoke renegotiation with a "captive" local public authority in the future (low balling strategy) (Chong, Huet and Saussier, 2006). Significantly as well, public-private partnerships are not immune to collusion and corruption strategies, especially because they usually deal with high-value contracts. This makes such contracts particularly prone to political contestability issues (Spiller, 2009), explaining why they usually appear to be very rigid – unable to be adapted to an evolving environment (see for example the difficulties encountered by English schools in order to change menus after Jamie Oliver's television show urging for a better food for children (Lawrence and Quarmby, 2005). Renegotiation may also occur because conditions change over the duration of a contract, necessitating an efficient adaptation mechanism for its terms (Estache and Saussier, 2014).

Public authorities also face switching costs in changing suppliers that induce them to stick with an inferior operator that was awarded a franchise. If a public authority switches suppliers, it could face political embarrassment and service interruption, reduced incentives for private parties to invest (fearing early contract termination), and would need to organise a new (costly) auction. On the flip side, these switching costs give firms incentive to renegotiate contracts to obtain higher prices, misrepresent costs, and provide low-quality service (to the extent that this behaviour is not monitored and/or that quality is not perfectly contractible). The problems that stem from imperfect and asymmetric information are even greater if the incumbent creates knowledge-specific capital that gives him/her a cost advantage.

Theory thus suggests that PPPs are plagued by difficulties that are not easily managed by (local) public authorities, who often require resources in order to manage the selection and contract execution processes. The capabilities required to manage PPPs are much more difficult to acquire for subnational governments than traditional procurement capacities.

What do we observe?

Public-private partnerships are not very popular in France – even if, paradoxically, concessions are widely used and have been for a long time. They are regularly criticised by French newspapers as being too expensive (see for example the advice given by the French Competition Authority concerning French concession contracts for highways – Avis 14-A-13, September 2014 – which was widely echoed and commented in the press[1]) and used in order to circumvent debt constraints.[2] In addition, some PPPs have been hit by corruption scandals (see for example the Balardgone case, an availability-based PPP launched in order to build and manage Paris buildings that are welcoming civil servants from the Defence department).[3] This is also the case for some public procurement contracts but PPPs are more frequently targeted by the news media. PPPs are also considered a political topic, their use being associated to greater or lesser degrees with political parties or political preferences, evidenced when looking at how availability-based contracts evolved in France (Box 2.1).

Box 2.1. The Caen Regional Multimedia Library: The influence of the state and regional levels

The Caen Regional Multimedia Library, financed through traditional procurement, opened in 2016 to replace the existing, outdated library in Caen. The new library was designed by Rem Koolhaas (who received the Golden Lion Award in the Venice Architecture Biennale in 2010) and is located in the city centre. The project started in 2010 and cost EUR 61 million, but the city will only have to pay EUR 40 million because the project benefits from EUR 21 million in subsidies from the national and regional levels of government. Many people have questioned the social value of such an investment and the choice made to locate the library in the city centre, especially considering recent technological evolutions that are reducing the need for people to physically be at the library to access books, newspapers, etc.

Source: Dagorn, Gary and Élise Delanoë (2014), "La future BMVR est-elle justifiée ?", *Mon Caen*, 21 February.

These elements suggest that PPPs are not always well managed by the (local) public authorities. In what follows, we focus on two case studies of cities, one medium-sized and one large, to highlight the difficulties associated with PPPs at the local level, and the solutions that could be implemented to address them.

Subnational PPPs

The case of Caen

The use of PPPs in Caen

Caen is the prefecture of the Calvados department and the capital of the Normandy region. The city has 108 365 inhabitants (as of 2012 national census), while its functional urban area has 420 000 inhabitants, making Caen the largest city in Lower Normandy. The urban area of Caen, in turn, is the second largest in Normandy after that of Rouen, the 21st largest in France.

The city has adopted a mixed approach to the organisation of its public services. Some services are contracted out; the majority of them are publicly managed by the city. Infrastructure needs for the city are globally met. There is a multi-year strategic plan decided at the city level – which is an obligation for French cities. Only very few shortages were mentioned during interviews. This is because the city is mainly responsible for infrastructure investments. With the exception of national and department roads (that are not important for the city of Caen), the city decides unilaterally. When the investment is decided at the urban area level, the city of Caen is the main actor, deciding where and how to invest. There is no issue of mismatch nor overlap with other decision-making levels, nor are there laws or regulations that might interfere at different levels of government. The only interference comes from the fact that some regional investments are subsidised by the state, influencing investment decisions that are taken at the regional level. Some investments that are not a priority might be favoured as soon as the city or the urban area want to benefit from subsides (e.g. the Caen Regional Multimedia Library, Box 2.1.).

Infrastructure needs in Caen are mainly achieved through traditional public procurement, not PPPs (Table 2.1). When concession contracts are signed, they are often lease contracts involving few private investments (i.e. the private partner is mainly involved in the operation phase and may invest for maintenance, but not in the construction phase). According to our interviews, the main reasons why the city decided to develop PPPs were to decrease the delivery time for primary infrastructure and to increase the efficiency during the operation phase. Those motives are in line with previous studies on French PPP contracts. Saussier and Tran (2012) showed that 77% of availability-based contracts delivered infrastructure on time in France. Conditional payments to the private partner are a strong driver in achieving such a good result. In addition, another reason put forward is that when revenue budgets are under pressure, public authorities can decide to make short-term savings by cutting the cost of ongoing maintenance of infrastructure assets. This might lead to increased costs overall as the costs of delayed maintenance can greatly exceed regular, more timely, maintenance. It can also decrease the quality level of the provided services. By contrast, in a PPP, because the private partner is contractually obliged to maintain the infrastructure (and encouraged to do so in concession contracts), the procuring authority is contractually obliged to pay for it and the efficiency during the operation phase is increased.

Table 2.1. Services contracted out in Caen

Services contracted out	Type of contract	Partner	Private %	Decision level
Water distribution	Concession (Lease)	Private / Veolia	100	City
Peace Memorial	Concession (Lease)	Public-private local public company (LPE)	<50	City
Equestrian Centre	Concession (Lease)	Private	100	City
Crematorium	Concession (Lease)	Private	100	City
Exhibition Hall	Concession (Lease)	Private	100	City
Heating network	Concession	Private - Dalkia	100	City
Car parks	Concession	Private - Vinci	100	City
Zenith – Music Hall	Concession	Public-private LPE	<50	City
Airport	Concession	Private – Chamber of Commerce and Industry	100	Urban area
SeaPort	Concession	Private	100	City
Waste management	Concession (Lease)	Private	100	Urban area
Court of Justice	Availability-based	Private	100	State
IT network	Concession	Private	100	Urban area
Hospital	Availability-based	Private - Bouygues	100	Urban area
Golf	Concession (Lease)	Private	100	Urban area
Vehicle pound	Concession (Lease)	Private	100	City
Tourism Office	Concession (Lease)	Private	100	City / Urban area

Source: Recollection by the authors from interviews made at the city level.

Caen's experience with PPPs has been mixed. An availability-based contract signed by the urban area for the creation of the Caen Hospital Centre proved problematic at early stages. Inadequate public sector capabilities at the outset of the project hampered the implementation of the PPP. The resulting experience partially explains why such contracts have not been used more broadly by the city and highlights how a past experience may have long-lasting effect.

Problems with hospital PPPs are not unique to the urban area of Caen. In its 2014 report, the French Court of Auditors (Cour des Comptes)[4] devotes a full chapter to public-private partnerships (PPPs) for hospitals. The Court wrote, "these proceedings were launched precipitously, the benefits that are attributed to PPPs were poorly exploited and financial issues have been insufficiently taken into account." The report pointed out that 24 hospitals were conducted in PPPs for an investment of EUR 613 million and that there was no real choice made by public authorities to go through PPPs or other procedures. PPPs have been "deployed in haste without the accompanying legal tools and management institutions are sufficiently available."

Concerning the choice of the PPP, the Court regrets that "no prior study has actually been required, neither on the financial implications of the project, nor in terms of comparison with the public project contracting procedure." The Court believes that "the lack of sufficient preparation for this new procedure, inexperience and the negotiators largely oriented assistance for PPPs led to the selection of disparate operations and the signing of contracts holders of financial uncertainty."

Concerning the contractual side, safeguard contractual provisions to ensure the continuity of public service have been incorporated into many contracts with a set of financial penalties applicable in case of unavailability of each function essential to the hospital. But the Court pointed out that "some are not sufficient," and "contracts reviewed did not sufficiently cover the diversity of conflicts that can arise in a period of 18-30 years […] A balance must be struck between the stability of the contract that brings financial security and the necessary amendments to the evolution of medical practices. This is one source of the inherent complexity of hospital PPPs." This balance is not easy to find for public authorities that lack contractual capabilities.

The difficulties encountered in availability-based contracts arising from a lack of contractual capabilities on the part of local authorities are also encountered in concession contracts, as the Caen tram network example illustrates (Box 2.2).

Box 2.2. The Caen guided light transit (Tram)

The Caen guided light transit (Tram) project involved 24 three-section articulated vehicles, guided by a central non-supporting rail, to provide service. The entire passenger line is guided, and in normal service, the vehicles are powered by electricity drawn from an overhead wire through a pantograph. After a construction period of three years, the system opened on 18 November 2002 with a total cost of EUR 227 million.

This project was organised through two 30-year concession contracts: one for the construction part of the project and one for the service part of the project. Many problems appeared during the execution phase of the contract because the two private partners took advantage of their informational advantage compared to the public authority. As soon as unexpected events/performance issues arose, it was impossible to clearly delineate which partner was responsible. With three major breakdowns per day, a rate 32 times higher than the contractual objective, above normal maintenance costs of EUR 1 million per year and penalties of EUR 1.5 million paid by both concessionaires for nine years, it is fair to say that the tram did not bring the expected results.

Due to its unreliability, the Caen urban area confirmed its plans to abandon the Caen TVR in favour of light rail by 2018. The light rail is set to take 18 months to construct and has an approximately EUR 170 million price tag. The conversion to light rail also means the termination of two concession contracts that Keolis and Bombardier-Spie Batignolles consortium STVR hold. Faced with possible appeals, Viacités – the transport union of the Caen urban area – will also apply to the administrative court for the appointment of an expert, in order to establish the level of responsibility of the STVR. In late 2014, the French government pledged EUR 23.3 million towards Caen's light rail conversion project, which is now expected to cost approximately EUR 230 million.

Source: Leguel, P. and P. Ambrosi (2011), "Caen abandonne l'exploitation du tramway sur pneus avant son terme", *Les Echos*, 19 December; Tramways and Urban Transit, January 2003; Ian Allan Publishing/Light Rail Transit Association.

What would facilitate the development of PPPs in Caen?

Despite being a dynamic French city, Caen, like other cities, has limited familiarity with PPPs. Having no specialised personnel for PPPs, the city is characterised by a lack of expertise and capabilities to manage them, from the award procedure to the end of the contract execution. Even if some examples of success in PPPs are cited during interviews - for example the case of the Caen Memorial Museum (Box 2.3) – those successes are not easy and necessitate a real human-capital investment from the city, in order to negotiate and follow the contract, sometimes renegotiating it in order to improve its efficiency like in the case of the Caen Memorial Museum (for which renegotiations were easy to manage because of the involved partner), cf. Table 2.1.

Box 2.3. The Caen Memorial Museum, Centre for History and Peace

In 1988, the Caen Memorial Museum, Centre for History and Peace, opened its doors. The infrastructure has been entirely built using public funds but the operating expenses (renewal of exploitation material and equipment) have been borne by a semi-public company (Société d'Economie Mixte, SEM) of which the city of Caen is the majority shareholder.

Because of a decline in the number of visitors, the city decided in 1997 to invest in the memorial extension to allow for a diversification of the themes addressed. However, anticipating that this new investment may generate generous extra revenue for the SEM, in 2002, the city has renegotiated the contract to compel the SEM to pay a rent to the city for occupying the place, just before the extension was open to the public.

In its 2014 annual report, the *Cour des Comptes* criticised the way the city of Caen subsidised the SEM. When looking at the financial reports from 1996 to 2001 (except in 1997), the SEM achieved a negative operating result each year, and was only positively balanced due to extraordinary results originating from the granted subsidies. There were two main sources of subsidies namely, a compensation for the gratuity of cultural services and discount rate for specific groups of individuals (e.g. students, seniors), and the renewal of equipment. Two main reproaches were made regarding the way the discount rates were compensated. First, it was based on the lower range of the expected number of visitors and therefore could leave some rents to the SEM. Second, the difference between the compensated tariff and the full-rate tariff was so low that the SEM did not get the proper incentives to make efforts to attract full-rate visitors, and it was also against the principle of reporting the risk of demand to the SEM. Also, the city subsidised spending that should have technically been imputed to the SEM (e.g. the national communication campaign, museum curator).

However, it is important to keep in mind that the Caen Memorial Museum is a cultural institution and is still an example of good management in the sector. Indeed, even though the amount of subsidies was important, it was relatively low compared to similar museums and its level was constantly declining before the extension opening. In addition, the revenue generated by the museum was also relatively high for the cultural sector. It is also worth noting that renegotiation could be favourable to the public entity, as was the case when the city of Caen decided to collect a rent for the usage of the installation after the extension of the museum was realised.

Source: Various sources, including interviews and Cour des Comptes (2014), *Rapport public annuel de la Cour des comptes - 2014*.

Capabilities needed by the city to run public services are different from those required to manage PPPs. Such capabilities are not easy to develop, especially in a short period. Public authorities can learn from accumulating experiences over time and through various situations. That is why what frequently comes up when discussing such issues with public authorities is the need for a national or regional observatory[5] accumulating data and experience in order to diffuse information about what is working and what is not working well with PPPs. This observatory could also support cities in deciding whether or not to opt for PPPs, in the implementation of the call for bids, as well as in the contractual details. However, our interviews suggest that such an observatory should not be considered as a third party involved in the city's decision to invest because cities are independent and feel strongly about their independence. That is why such third-party involvement could be more easily implemented during the execution stage (which is, theoretically, an important stage where renegotiations take place and might be very costly) and might be welcomed for complex infrastructure projects.

Interviews also suggest that more clear guidance from the national government and a stable regulatory environment regarding the use of PPPs are essential. More broadly, at the European level, discussions concerning the new European Directive on Concessions illustrate the divergence among European countries on this issue (Box 1.1).

The case of Paris

The use of PPPs in Paris

The case of Paris is interesting because, unlike Caen, the city is familiar with PPP contracts and has a dedicated staff unit for such PPPs. The city is most familiar with concession contracts, with 182 that are ongoing. In 2013, they represented a turnover of EUR 1.5 billion. Some of those contracts are signed with local public enterprises (LPEs). LPEs are mainly present for car parks, funerary services, district heating, cold energy, Eiffel Tower management as well as the management of the POPB (Paris-Bercy Stadium). Concessions managed by LPEs represent a global turnover of EUR 572 million (one-third of concessions total turnover). Figure 2.3. shows the repartition of activities for which concessions were used in Paris.

Figure 2.3. Concessions turnover in Paris City, 2013

EUR millions

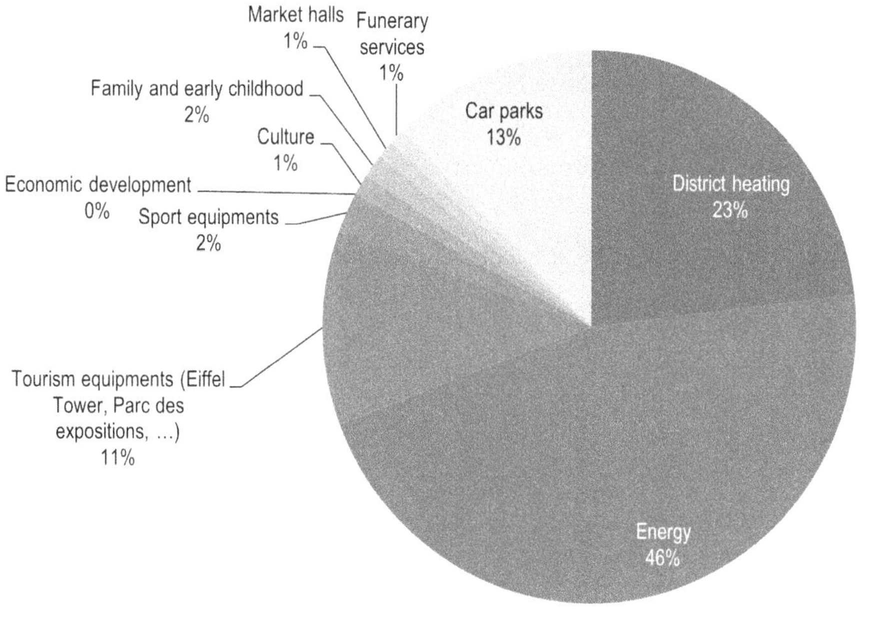

Source: Based on Paris City document 2015-DFA-79.

The city of Paris' experience with availability-based contracts is considerably more limited: only one has been signed by the city. This single contract is part of the city's Climate Plan adopted in 2007. The city of Paris is committed to reducing the energy consumption and greenhouse gas emissions of its public buildings by 30% before 2020. This commitment involves the refurbishing of 600 schools in Paris. A first group of 100 schools was selected for renovation through an availability-based contract. With nearly EUR 50 million in investment, it is one of France's largest energy renovation programmes. It was launched in 2011, and by 2014, performance goals were achieved for 45 of the 100 schools targeted for the first round of work performed, with a 33% reduction of energy consumption and 34% of greenhouse gas emissions. The results exceeded expected objectives (Khalid, 2014). However, the city decided to continue refurbishing the remaining 500 schools using traditional procurement contracts instead of availability-based PPPs. This is because of: 1) a new French legislation opening the path for global public procurement contract linking investments and service provision in a single contract (which was not allowed before 2011); and 2) the legislative complexity of using availability-based contracts. The difference between both types of contractual agreements is mainly derived from the fact that the payment is delayed in an availability-based contract and not allowed in a (global) public procurement contract.

Infrastructure needs and main reasons to use PPPs in Paris

The case of Paris is interesting because, contrary to that of Caen, the city is familiar with concession contracts and has staff dedicated to such activity. However, even with such experience, the city is going back and forth in some activities (e.g. water) and is experiencing difficulties regardless of the type of operator: private or semi-public (see Box 2.4, Box 2.5 and Box 2.6). This shows that concessions with private partners as well as with semi-public concessionaires have their problems. Some are common (e.g. difficulty in controlling the concessionaire and receiving data). Others seem more specific to semi-public concessionaires, such as the low level of effort placed in adapting to demand, as well as financial difficulties.

Box 2.4. The case of the Vélib'

The *Vélib'* case is an interesting illustration of the pitfalls associated with public-private contracting highlighted by contract theories (Williamson, 1976; Hart, Shleifer and Vishny, 1997, Laffont and Tirole, 1993). In 2006, the city of Paris decided to provide a bicycle-sharing programme to its citizens – the *Vélib'*. In exchange for city billboards, private companies bid in order to provide the bicycle service. The call for bids was difficult to organise. In a first round, Clear Channel won, offering 14 000 bikes instead of the 7 500 bikes proposed by its competitor JC Decaux. However, after a judicial appeal, the city was obliged to reorganise a call for bids. The second round was won by JC Decaux, which offered 20 00 bikes. An investment of more than EUR 80 million was planned over the ten-year contract period.

During the execution stage of the contract, it became clear that the contract was not adapted and renegotiations occurred. Penalties for late deployment of the bikes were not applied, as is often the case for public-private contracts (Saussier and Tirole, 2015). Performance indicators were badly chosen: for example, the private company was responsible for monitoring the bike network to ensure that a user would find at least one bike at each station. One way to reach this performance level was for JC Decaux to leave a broken bike in each station (see CRC report, 2012). On top of this, JC Decaux had no financial incentive to provide a service of good quality because the user fees were going back to the city. Finally, vandalism was underestimated in the initial contract (61% of the bike fleet deteriorated during the first year of operation) leading the city to accept a renegotiation in 2007 and again 2009, paying EUR 400 per stolen bike over a threshold since 2009. An interesting detail illustrating asymmetric information issues is that the city found out, two years after accepting to renegotiate that more than 70% of the stolen bikes were found by the company and put back into the system, leading the city to pay several times for the same bike.

Renegotiations that occurred also changed the nature of the initial contract by providing incentives to JC Decaux to increase the number of users of the *Vélib'*. After 2009, the company kept 35% of the net turnover as soon as it went over EUR 14 million and 50% as soon as it reached more than EUR 17.5 million. The initial public procurement contract moved toward a concession contract where the private company was paid directly by the users.

The *Vélib'* contract ended in 2017 and the city re-opened a call for tender. This time the city opted for a concession contract instead of a public procurement contract.

Source: Rapport de la Chambre Régionale des Comptes (CRC) d'Ile-de-France – June 2012; Inspection Générale Ville de Paris, Audit du contrat Velib, 2016; *Les Echos*, 12 April 2017.

Box 2.5. Car park concessions in Paris

Private operator

In 2010, the city of Paris conducted an audit of car parks allocated through concession contracts to the private operator Vinci Park. This is main concessionaire in Paris, with more than 90 parks under its responsibility for a total turnover of EUR 117 million per year (out of the EUR 175 million generated for all car parks organised through concessions in Paris). The report concludes that there is a lack of co-ordination between the city and Vinci Park; that information is asymmetric in favour of Vinci; and that concession contracts appear to be too rigid for the city to adapt to its strategy (i.e. the environmental strategy of the city would be strengthened by an increase of car park services but such an increase would favour Vinci Park too much as they were not anticipated in the long-term contracts). The main conclusion of the report is that the city, in order to recover its control over the public service, should revert to direct public management by not renewing the concession contracts when they expire.

The report stated, "The Audit recommends more exchanges between the City and the private operator to allow the City to ensure a better control of its parks and greater mastery of the pricing policy. The audit has indeed led to identify the existence in some parks entrusted to Vinci Park specific price schemes that deserved to be brought to the attention of the City." This exemplifies the fact that concessions are incomplete contracts and that the private operator might decide some prices (toward specific clients) not envisioned by the city.

The report also stated the need to renegotiate "oldest car parks concession contracts in the inner city. Higher hourly rates can only take place at the initiative of the public authorities. They would represent, in the current situation, a financial advantage for the private operator that is difficult to justify. The new pricing policy implies the renegotiation of the financial terms of concession contracts of the oldest parks in the inner city." This exemplifies the fact that concession contracts are incomplete but also too rigid, as they impede Paris from ensuring that car park prices evolve as the city wishes without costly renegotiations with the private operator.

Semi-private company

In 2013, the city of Paris audited car parks allocated through concession contracts to a local semi-public enterprise: the SAEMES. The SAEMES is in charge of 41 car parks in Paris, corresponding to 21% of parking places in the city. The report states that the profitability of the SAEMES is burdened by significant investments that are generating little revenues. Some 18 of 41 parks are structurally in loss, among which 6 have a negative gross operating profit. This contrasts with car parks operated by Vinci Park (above) for which 9 of 66 contracts appear structurally in loss including 5 contracts generating a negative gross operating profit. The report also states that SAEMES lacks the necessary tools to anticipate risks and to measure the impact of new management and financial decisions.

The report notes that the city would like to control the SAEMES' investment renewal programme, in particular to know the number of failures recorded in the SAEMES' car parks and their impact in terms of discomfort or unavailability. However SAEMES considers direct consultation of its computerised maintenance management software by the city as incompatible with the principle of a concession and refuses to let the city access it.

The report also found that in some parks the system that displays information did not work and that in general the company had little or limited equipment that was up to date technologically (plasma information screens, etc.). More broadly, few efforts were made to develop the brand name of the SAEMES and to respond to customer complaints.

Finally, since 2003 all maintenance projects have run behind the schedule set in the initial agreements. Neither the time nor the costs estimated during the bidding phase have been met. While the slippage of costs is only detrimental to SAEMES and its shareholders – at least in the short term – in the long run renegotiations may occur, passing costs to user fees - missing deadlines also penalises the users.

Sources: Audit des DSP des Parcs de stationnement confiées à la société Vinci – Inspection Générale de la Ville de Paris, 2010 (www.paris.fr/municipalite/l-hotel-de-ville/evaluation-inspection-generale-183#audit-des-dsp-des-parcs-de-stationnement-confiees-a-la-societe-vinci); Audit du Train de vie de la SAEMES – Inspection Générale de la Ville de Paris, 2013 (www.paris.fr/municipalite/l-hotel-de-ville/evaluation-inspection-generale-183#audit-du-train-de-vie-de-la-saemes).

Interestingly, even if the city of Paris has experience with respect to concessions, some difficulties still occur – as illustrated by the case of Ternes car park (Box 2.6).

Box 2.6. The case of the Ternes car park

In February 2002, the city decided to renew its concession contract for the "Ternes" car park. The winner, Omniparc, a society belonging to Eiffage, one of the major players in the field (together with Vinci), won the 12-year-long contract. The contract mentioned the need to renovate and extend the capacity of the car park (280 parking spaces in addition to the 1 336 existing ones), with a cost of more than EUR 13 million (EUR 8 million for the extension) for the new concessionaire.

Work was supposed to start within 18 months of the contract's signature. The concessionaire began renovating the park and argued that it cost EUR 8 million instead of the EUR 5 million initially anticipated. The concessionaire refused to invest more in order to extend the capacity of the park contrary to the contractual agreement. The company asked for a renegotiation of the initial contract arguing that costs were underestimated and needed to be increase to EUR 15 million instead of the EUR 8 million initially anticipated. The reasons invoked were that new security legislation showed up and induced the need to amortise investment in a shorter period than was expected. The city refused to renegotiate and to pay more than initially agreed.

In October 2008, the city ordered the concessionaire to start the contractually agreed project. When the concessionaire did not do so, the city terminated the contract (in 2009), without any compensation for the concessionaire. The concessionaire sued the city, requesting that the termination be cancelled, arguing that investment had been underestimated and that the city should not have accepted to sign a contract with such an unreasonably low offer. On its side, the city asked for EUR 12 million as indemnities for damages due to bad quality service over the period the concessionaire operated the car park. The administrative court ruled in favour of the city in June 2011, but only required the concessionaire to pay EUR 27 000 in damages to the city. The car park is now operated through a concession contract with another concessionaire (Autocité – Spie batignolles).

Source: Saussier (2017) Public-private partnerships for infrastructure at the subnational level of government: Opportunities and challenges in France and http://www.chaire-eppp.org/wp-content/uploads/2018/04/saussier-2017.pdf.

Several points are worth noting in the Ternes car park case. First, it illustrates the now well-known low-balling strategy used by concessionaires to bid very aggressively, anticipating that they will succeed in renegotiating the initial contract to their advantage *ex post*. Second, such conflicts are usually rare as the public authorities often accept to renegotiate or the concessionaire accepts not to renegotiate in order to preserve its reputation (sometimes by reducing costs and decreasing quality). This was not the case here, probably because of a change in Omniparc ownership in 2008, when it was purchased by Q-Park. This company was not at the origin of the offer and this might explain their reluctance to invest so much money in the park. Another explanation is also that the city of Paris is more experienced than other public authorities and can be credible when saying there will be no renegotiation (however the *Vélib'* case contradicts this view; see Box 2.4).

However, as is the case for the city of Caen, it appears that PPPs require that cities invest in and develop their capabilities to manage every step of the agreement, from the award procedure to the execution stage. Such difficulties, as well as the fact that PPPs are susceptible to challenge by political opponents, may explain why the city questions the value of PPPs, going back and forth sometimes – for water services for example. This implies the need to involve all the stakeholders at every step of the PPP process to avoid third-party opportunism(Spiller, 2009), which can take the form of political challenges that destabilise PPPs. The new governance for PPPs that was put in place in Paris at the end of 2014 can be considered an organisational innovation designed to cope with these issues (Box 2.7).

Box 2.7. A new governance for public-private partnerships in Paris

In September 2014, the city of Paris set up new governance bodies for concessions with high stakes: the Board of Concessions and the Commission of Elected People.

The Board of Concessions is a concession steering body responsible for defining the strategic objectives, upstream of award procedures but also at the renewal stage of emblematic or strategic city's concessions. Its remit covers the concessions at large. It includes public procurement contracts with forgone revenues (e.g. Vélib' or Paris' kiosks[1]) and availability-based contracts. Its composition has a variable geometry but it comprises all stakeholders and decision makers concerned with the agenda: alongside the Secretary General of the Directorate of Finance and Procurement and Legal Affairs Department, the contract managers' directions, sometimes some elected officials are invited to participate. The board thus constitutes a prior arbitration body and defines a strategy with a must at key stages of the contracts' procedure.

The Commission of Elected People consists of nine elected permanent members. Members are carefully chosen, notably in order to represent the elected representatives of the political opposition. The commission meets to set up some guidelines in the case of procurement procedures or particular strategic or symbolic contract renewals. Meetings in this commission anticipate the ones of the Paris Council since the Commission considers well before awarding contracts, the project, the proposed management methods, terms of competition and the award criteria.

It is expected that these two bodies will address those strategic issues for contracts that are not necessarily with significant stakes in financial terms. The final objectives of these bodies are essentially to:

- Increase transparency in the management of public services;
- Modernise and secure the award procedures and implementation of public-private partnerships around a "standard city", with the aim of drafting a guide for the main financial provisions being found in all concession contracts; and
- Involve elected upstream of the decision and contract renewals.

The set-up of this new governance illustrates (political) difficulties encountered by the city concerning the development of PPPs. However, since this new governance system has been in place, little communication has been undertaken by the city concerning its decisions and its efficiency.

Note: Public procurement contracts with forgone revenues are contractual arrangements that are similar to concessions. For example, the Velib' is a traditional procurement contract signed between the city and JC Decaux (see Box 2.4). In exchange for investing and operating the service, JC Decaux received the right to operate for free the city's billboards, for which the city foregoes revenues.

Source: Saussier (2017) Public-private partnerships for infrastructure at the subnational level of government: Opportunities and challenges in France and http://www.chaire-eppp.org/wp-content/uploads/2018/04/saussier-2017.pdf.

Lessons

PPPs are long-term (incomplete) contractual agreements. As such, they are plagued by transaction costs. Those costs depend on several elements:

- **Contractual choices**: Cities need to develop contractual capabilities in order to properly design their contracts, knowing that they face private companies that are used to contracts and that the devil is often in the detail (Brown and Potoski, 2003);
- **Governance choices**: Cities need to think carefully about the kind of PPPs that is appropriate for their infrastructure and service needs. Availability-based and concession contracts are sometimes alternative solutions but should be evaluated before signature and confronted as well with the traditional procurement solution (this last point is often forgotten); and
- **Institutional frameworks**: Cities need to make their choices in a secured and stable environment. Even better, this environment can provide help for them to develop or have access to relevant capabilities in order to sign successful PPPs.

PPPs are costly partnerships with a political dimension

The two cases presented here – Caen and Paris – offer several lessons. The first lesson is that PPPs are costly partnerships. PPPs can be associated with expectations that responsibilities/agreements will be met. However, cities must be aware that these expectations come with a cost. Because PPPs are long-term contracts, they are also characterised by transaction costs (Williamson, 1985) that the city should try to minimise. This is not an easy process. Asymmetric information exists between public and private parties, often to the advantage of private ones. In addition, and reinforcing this position of weakness, public authorities usually lack contractual capabilities because they differ from those needed to run public services through traditional procurement. Such difficulties are not insurmountable. As illustrated by the case of Aquanova (Box 2.8), even a small city can develop a new infrastructure through PPPs at the cost of investing a lot in the contractual process and details.

Box 2.8. The case of Aquanova: Challenges in the implementation of an availability-based contract in a small city

Aquanova is an aquatic centre financed through an availability-based contract at Saint-Dié-des-Vosges, a small city of 21 000 inhabitants. This project illustrates that even a small city can use PPPs but it has to be supported by strong political will and significant administrative investment. The EUR 18.5 million project (EUR 12 million investments) started in June 2012 and was completed in early January 2014. At the beginning, the city considered using a concession contract to finance the project, but after a year of discussions, it opted for an availability-based contract. The result was an aquatic centre offering multiple new services compared to the previous swimming pool but for the same price. It groups multiple services (e.g. swimming pool, diving pool, massages, fitness centre) with sustainable development objectives in a region where household revenues are low. Some 82% of the revenues generated by this project are subject to added value taxes, generating substantial revenue for the city. Thus far, the project has been considered a success.

Source: Interviews and *Vosges Matin* (2016), "Les succès d'AquaNova America", 20 November, www.vosgesmatin.fr/edition-de-saint-die/2016/11/20/les-succes-d-aquanova-america.

Even when the city developed such capabilities, because PPPs are complex contracts, they come at a cost, opening the door to criticism. Such objections usually forget that alternative arrangements (i.e. traditional procurement) are not immune to other limits – not studied in this chapter – potentially even more costly for cities. Nevertheless, they might destabilise the willingness of the city to develop PPPs.

In addition, PPPs are characterised by the importance of the institutional environment. PPP legislation is not considered as secured by parties: availability-based contracts were launched in June 2004 and as such constitute an organisational innovation. Since then, a new law modified the legislation around those PPPs in July 2008 and the legislation evolved again with the translation into national law of the public procurement European Directive 2014/24/UE.[6] These evolutions do not provide a stable institutional environment for contracting parties.

Lastly, PPPs are public-private agreements, characterised by the importance of the political dimension. As pointed out by Spiller (2009), "A fundamental difference between private and public contracts is that public contracts are in the public sphere, and thus, although politics is normally not necessary to understand private contracting, it becomes fundamental to understanding public contracting." Hence, a large part of the control is done by third parties (e.g. stakeholders, consumer associations, political contesters) that are not necessarily interested in the success of the agreement and that might look to destabilise it (Beuve, Moszoro, and Saussier, 2015) and the political agenda is an issue that might destabilise PPPs, especially around election times (Le Squeren, 2016).

The need for public contracting capacity

One of the main avenues for developing PPPs is to provide cities with the knowledge needed to cope with PPP challenges. Because PPPs are considered for many cities as an "organisational innovation", many of them are reluctant to develop them, waiting for others to start.

One way to provide cities with the needed knowledge and capability would be to put in place a national observatory in charge of collecting data on PPPs signed all over the country as well as traditional public procurement contracts. This observatory could advise cities in their choices of organisational arrangement for their infrastructures and could also be in charge of following PPPs' performances once they are signed. In addition to strengthening capabilities, such an observatory could increase the level of transparency around PPPs and consequently the accountability of public decision makers.

In their note to the French government, Saussier and Tirole (2015) emphasised that a greater monitoring of public expenses is needed. They suggest that it could take the form, for high amount contracts whatever their form (i.e. traditional public procurement, concession or availability-based contracts), of a prior evaluation systematically performed, including the full cost and anticipated advantages for each project. These prior evaluations would make it possible to identify the most appropriate form of contract to meet the public need. They also suggest that such an observatory could also collect information about the contract execution stage, especially renegotiations. This point seems particularly important with the translation of European Directives in early 2016, allowing large renegotiations without being clear about how to monitor them. In addition to the relevant players being held accountable, such information would make it possible to compare the conditions under which contracts are executed, along with the conclusions drawn from studies performed at the pre-contractual stage and that have resulted in one method of procurement being chosen over another. Such evaluations should be carried out by a national observatory, which would also facilitate the centralisation of data and results and the possibility of comparing the best contractual practices.

Such a collection of data and information concerning PPPs and traditional public procurement contracts signed in France would also allow for an objective picture of PPPs' performances, helping to reduce political contestability and to stabilise the institutional framework. Ideally, it should be extended to complex traditional public procurement contracts. The need for such an observatory is suggested by the European Directives on public procurement and concession contracts.

A PPP task force, the Mission d'appui aux PPP (MAPPP), was created in 2004 but had been limited to availability-based contracts. Since April 2016, this task force has been replaced by another, the Mission d'appui au Financement des Infrastructures (Fin Infra) with more responsibilities. In particular, its mission was extended to every kind of complex public private contracts. The objective is to standardise market practices by spreading the knowledge of adequate allocation of risks for bankable projects among public clients. For such an observatory to succeed, a considerable budget will be needed for these objectives to be fulfilled.

Notes

1. See: www.autoritedelaconcurrence.fr/user/standard.php?id_rub=592&id_article=2429&lang=en.
2. See, for example, the report from two French Senators - Les contrats de partenariats: Des bombes à retardement? - Rapport d'information n° 733 (2013-2014) by Mr. Jean-Pierre Sueur and Mr. Hugues Portelli, 16 July 2014, available at www.senat.fr/rap/r13-733/r13-733_mono.html.
3. See, for example, Le Monde and AFP (2014).
4. The Court of Auditors is a quasi-judicial body of the French government charged with conducting financial and legislative audits of most public institutions and some private institutions.
5. The number of French regions was reduced from 22 to 13 regions in France since January 2016. This may justify the creation of regional observatories that would benefit from scale economies and would be easier to create and manage with fewer regions.
6. Concession contracts are also touched by the translation in national law of the concession European Directive 2014/23/UE, but more lightly (see Saussier and Tirole, 2015).

References

Beuve, Jean, Marian W. Moszoro and Stéphane Saussier (2015), "Political Contestability and Contract Rigidity: An Analysis of Procurement Contracts", *SSRN Scholarly Paper*, Social Science Research Network, Rochester, NY, http://papers.ssrn.com/abstract=2475164.

Brown, Trevor L. and Matthew Potoski (2003), "Contract–management capacity in municipal and county governments", *Public Administration Review* 63(2), pp. 153–164.

Chong, Huet and Stéphane Saussier (2006), "Auctions, ex post competition and prices: The efficiency of public private partnerships", *Annuals of Public and Cooperative Economics*.

Cour des Comptes (2014), *Rapport public annuel de la Cour des comptes - 2014*.

Dagorn, Gary and Élise Delanoë (2014), "La future BMVR est-elle justifiée ?", *Mon Caen*, 21 February.

Estache, Antonio and Stéphane Saussier (2014), "public-private partnerships and efficiency: A short assessment", *CESifo DICE Report* 12(3), pp. 8-13.

Hart, Oliver, Andrei Shleifer and Robert W. Vishny (1997), "The proper scope of government: Theory and an application to prisons", *Quarterly Journal of Economics* 112(4), pp. 1 127–1 161.

Institu pour la Gestion Déléguée (2011), *Aspects économiques et comptables des investissements dans les PPP*.

Khalid, Nohmana (2014), "La rénovation énergétique des 500 écoles parisiennes ne se fera pas en PPP", LeMoniteur.fr, 31 October, www.lemoniteur.fr/article/la-renovation-energetique-des-500-ecoles-parisiennes-ne-se-fera-pas-en-ppp-26241333.

Laffont, Jean-Jacques and Jean Tirole (1993), *A Theory of Incentives in Procurement and Regulation*, MIT Press, Cambridge, MA.

Lawrence, Felicity and Katharine Quarmby (2005), "Private deals block Jamie's school dinners", *The Guardian*, 25 April, www.theguardian.com/society/2005/apr/25/schools.politics.

Leguel, P. and P. Ambrosi (2011), "Caen abandonne l'exploitation du tramway sur pneus avant son terme", *Les Echos*, 19 December.

Le Monde and AFP (2014), "Affaire du « Pentagone français » : deux hommes, dont un militaire, mis en examen", www.lemonde.fr/societe/article/2014/05/13/affaire-du-pentagone-francais-deux-hommes-dont-un-militaire-mis-en-examen_4416256_3224.html.

Le Squeren, Zoé (2016),"Politics and Public Administration: The Influence of Electoral Motives and Ideology on the Management of Local Public Services", thesis. https://tel.archives-ouvertes.fr/tel-01533699/document

OECD (2013), *Investing Together: Working Effectively across Levels of Government*, OECD Publishing, Paris, https://doi.org/10.1787/9789264197022-en.

OECD (2008) *Public-Private Partnerships: In Pursuit of Risk Sharing and Value for Money*, OECD Publishing, Paris, https://doi.org/10.1787/9789264046733-en.

Saussier, Stephane and Jean Tirole (2015), "Strengthening the Efficiency of Public Procurement", *Les notes du conseil d'analyse économique*, No. 22, April, www.cae-eco.fr/IMG/pdf/cae-note022-env2.pdf.

Saussier, Stéphane and Phuong Tra Tran (2012), "L'efficacité des contrats de partenariat en France : une première évaluation quantitative", *Revue d'économie industrielle* (140), pp. 81-110.

Spiller, Pablo T. (2009), "An institutional theory of public contracts: Regulatory implications", in Ménard, Claude and Michel Ghertman (eds.), *Regulation, Deregulation, Reregulation: Institutional Perspectives*, Edward Elgar.

Vosges Matin (2016), "Les succès d'AquaNova America", 20 November, www.vosgesmatin.fr/edition-de-saint-die/2016/11/20/les-succes-d-aquanova-america.

Williamson, Oliver E. (1985), *The Economic* Institutions *of Capitalism*, The Free Press, New York, NY.

Williamson, Oliver E. (1976), "Franchise bidding for natural monopolies: In general and with respect to CATV", *Bell Journal of Economics* 7(1), pp. 73–104.

Chapter 3. Public-private partnerships at the subnational level of government: The case of PFI in the United Kingdom

by Lee Mizell

This chapter presents a case study of public-private partnerships (PPPs) for infrastructure development in the United Kingdom (the UK). While PFI is now an historic mechanism, the UK's history with PFI and the limited attention to the regional and local government experience with PFI in existing literature make the experience at the subnational level particularly worthy of review. The case study explores four areas which can present challenges when implementing subnational public-private partnerships: 1) legal and regulatory arrangements; 2) financing and funding, 3) economies of scale, and 4) local administrative capacity. The case study concludes with a summary of lessons emerging from the UK's (and particularly England's) history with PFI at the subnational level.

Introduction

This chapter presents a case study of public-private partnerships (PPPs) for infrastructure development in the United Kingdom (the UK). More specifically, it examines subnational experience with a specific type of PPP – Private Finance Initiative (PFI) contracts with a focus on local authorities in England. Between 1997 and 2012, PFI was a key mechanism used to meet social infrastructure needs, particularly at the subnational level. In 2012, PFI was revised and replaced by PF2. While PFI is now an historic mechanism, the UK's history with PFI and the limited attention to the regional and local government experience with PFI in existing literature make the experience at the subnational level particularly worthy of review. The case study will address three main questions: 1) what trends can be observed with respect to PFI at the subnational levels of government over time? 2) how did multi-level governance arrangements play out with respect to local authority PFIs between 1997 and 2012 in England? and 3) what does the UK experience suggest in terms of governance of PPPs at the subnational level?

The case study is organised as follows. It begins with an historical overview of PFI in the UK, with a focus on England and the use of PFI at the local level. This is followed by a look at the multi-level governance context of subnational PFIs in the UK. In addition to a brief discussion of actors at different levels of government, it explores four areas which can present challenges when implementing subnational public-private partnerships: 1) legal and regulatory arrangements; 2) financing and funding, 3) economies of scale, and 4) local administrative capacity. The penultimate section provides a deeper examination of these issues by examining England's "Waste Infrastructure Delivery Programme" which emphasizes local PFI projects to help achieve EU landfill targets. The case study concludes with a summary of lessons emerging from the UK's (and particularly England's) history with PFI at the subnational level.

Background

Infrastructure needs and the emergence of PFI

At the outset of the 1980s, the UK's public sector owned the country's utilities and transportation, and owned and operated most social infrastructure such as schools and hospitals (Winch, 2012). This began to change in the 1980s as the country shifted toward increased private participation in infrastructure finance, ownership, and operation (Winch, 2012). Privatisation and concessions launched in the mid-1980s were followed by private finance in the 1990s (Winch, 2012).

The shift toward privatisation followed on the heels of substantial declines in public investment. Public investment as a percentage of GDP declined throughout the 1970s, and reached a first low point by the end of the 1980s before reaching an historical low at the end of the 1990s. Looking at gross capital formation as the measure of public investment, Clark et al. (2002) find a drop from 8.9% of GDP in 1975 to 1.7% in 2000. They attribute much of the dramatic decline in the 1970s to a substantial drop-off in local government investment, which fell from 3.8% of GDP in 1975 to 0.8% in 1982. Reduction in investment in council housing was the primary contributor in this regard. A second major contributor to the decline in public investment was effect of privatisation. Public corporations' contributions to GDP dropped from 2.8% of GDP in 1983 to 1.2% of GDP in 1988 to less than 0.5% in 2000 (Clark et al., 2002). According to the authors, there were also substantial declines in public investment in education. Finally, the 1990s saw declines in central government investment in general, which dropped from 1.4% of GDP in 1991 to 0.4% in 1999 (Clark et al., 2002). Clark et al. (2002: 307) argue that privatisation and declines in public investment were motivated by "a desire to contain the 'headline' measure of the public deficit — the public sector borrowing requirement (PSBR)" and to keep tax rates low in the face of rising non-discretionary expenditures such as social security. The historical trends can be observed in Figure 3.1., which tracks public sector net investment (slightly different from but based on gross fixed capital formation).

Figure 3.1. Public sector net investment as a % of GDP, 1948-2021

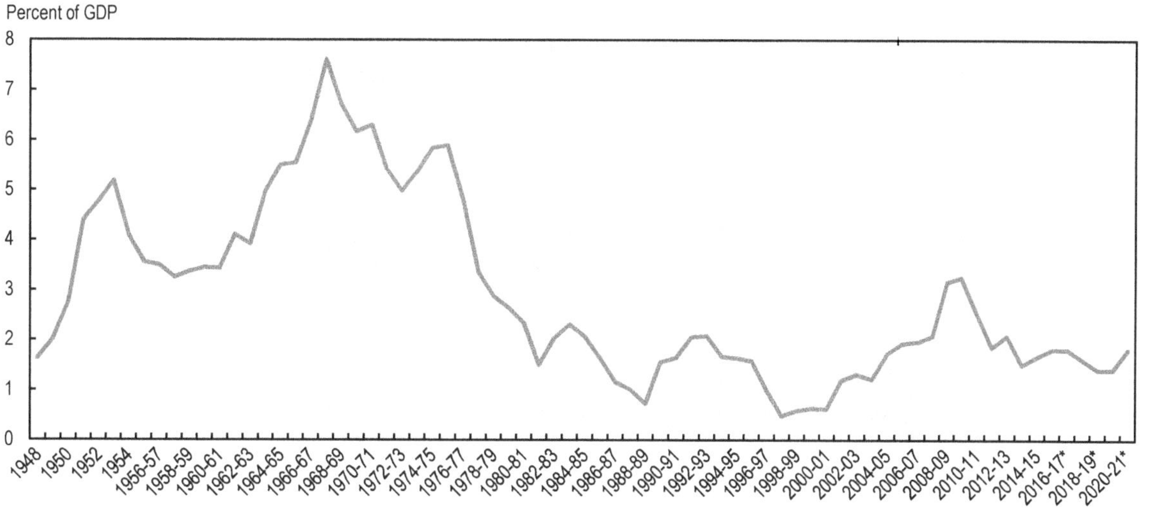

Note: Public Sector Net Investment is gross spending on investment less depreciation. Years with an asterisk are estimates.

Source: UK Office of Budget Responsibility (2015), PSF Aggregates Databank, Excel, November 2015.

By 1989, public investment was decidedly low in historical terms. Where the public sector did invest, it had a weak track record of delivering infrastructure projects on-time and on-budget, and tended to under invest in operations and maintenance (LexisPSL and Addleshaw Goddard, n.d.-a). To address some of these challenges, in 1992, the UK government formally launched the now well-known "Private Finance Initiative (PFI)", a special type of PPP, to help tackle infrastructure needs (Winch, 2012) (Box 3.1). Launched first with large central government projects (e.g. Channel Tunnel Rail Link and the Jubilee Line Extension), it was not until 1996/1997 that PFI was extended to subnational governments (Wilson and Game, 2011). The "Public Private Partnership Programme" (4ps, now called Local Partnerships) was established in 1996 to help extend PFI to local governments (Winch, 2012). Clark et al. (2002: 310) note that PFI was introduced at a time of "large and growing fiscal deficits" and thus at least partially justified by its positive impact on the public deficit (PBSR). From 1994 onward, HM Treasury approval for publicly funded capital investment was usually predicated on previous consideration of private finance options (House of Lords, 2010).

Box 3.1. PFI/PF2 vs. PPP

The UK's "Private Finance Initiative" was launched in 1992. While discussed in the context of public-private partnerships (PPPs/P3), PFI and PPP are not synonymous. PPP refers to a "family of procurement methods" (LexisPSL and Addleshaw Goddard, n.d.-a). By contrast, PFI is a specific type of PPP contract which bundles construction, operations, and maintenance into a single contract. The project is privately financed up-front via private sector equity and debt (usually debt), and paid for over the long-term with public funds. PFI traditionally involves establishing a Special Purpose Vehicle (SPV) to raise capital and undertake the project. The SPV is later repaid via fixed government payments (i.e. unitary charges) over the life of the project beginning in the operational phase. By contrast, a PPP need not involve such financing arrangements. PFI was replaced in December 2012 by similar but updated approach, Private Finance 2 (PF2) which will apply to England. New elements of PF2 include:

- Centralised procurement units for certain sectors;
- A maximum window of 18 months for the competitive tendering phase;
- Requirements that government act as a minority equity investor;
- Competitions for some portion of the private sector equity;
- A shift in risk allocation towards the public sector;
- Even greater standardisation of contract documents;
- The removal of soft facilities management from contracts; and
- Annual publication of project information, including off-balance sheet PF2 contract liabilities.

Despite the emergence of PF2, as PFI projects generally have a life span of approximately 25 years, numerous PFI projects are ongoing.

While PFI has tended to dominate public-private partnerships in the United Kingdom, it exists alongside other forms of PPPs.

Sources: LexisPSL and Addleshaw Goddard (n.d.-a), "Forms of Public Private Partnerships", LexisPSL Practice Note; LexisPSL and Addleshaw Goddard (n.d.-b), "Introduction to the Private Finance Initiative and Public Private Partnerships", LexisPSL Practice Note; LexisPSL and Laver, N. (2013), "PF2--the story so far", LexisPSL News Analysis; LexisPSL and Laver, N. (2012), "PF2--a new look for PFI?", LexisPSL News Analysis; HM Treasury (2012), "A new approach to public private partnerships", London, UK; EPEC (2012), "United Kingdom - England: PPP Units and Related Institutional Framework", European PPP Expertise Centre; House of Lords (2010), "Private Finance Projects and off-balance sheet debt, Volume I: Report", House of Lords Select Committee on Economic Affairs, 17 March 2010.

Transitioning to private finance of public infrastructure was not without hiccups. Early PFI deals were delayed by legal problems, costly and time-consuming bidding procedures, and weak public sector skills for this new, complex approach to procurement (Winch, 2012). Following the comprehensive government ("Bates") review in 1997, the government overhauled bidding procedures, clarified legal issues, and introduced a Treasury Taskforce to promote the PPP approach (Winch, 2012). A second review in 1999 led to the creation of Partnerships UK, a national "PPP unit" set up to promote PPPs and to provide technical support to HM Treasury and contracting authorities (Winch, 2012; OECD, 2015). As subsequent sections show, the PFI approach took off over the following decade.

While PFI achieved positive performance in some areas, there has also been criticism. Government reviews have suggested that PFI projects tend to outperform traditional procurement in terms of cost and schedule overruns (Winch, 2012). There is also an indication that maintenance is better managed under PFI than traditional procurement (House of Lords, 2010). Overall, PFI has likely facilitated infrastructure development that would not have been possible without private finance (Winch, 2012). However, emerging lessons attenuated some of the enthusiasm for PFI. Criticisms included inappropriate risk allocation, a lack of sufficient flexibility/difficulty to change contract terms, a lack of transparency regarding future liabilities, perceived excessive private sector profits, and lengthy and costly procurement (HM Treasury, 2012). In 2010, these criticisms, along with the effects of the 2008 financial crisis, prompted the incoming government to cancel significant PFI programmes underway and to undertake a review of PFI (LexisPSL and Addleshaw Goddard, n.d.-a). The result was the launch PF2 in 2012, a rebranded version of PFI with changes intended to improve value for money, increase procurement efficiency, introduce greater flexibility during the operational phase, and improve transparency and public confidence (LexisPSL and Addleshaw Goddard, n.d.-a; LexisPSL and Laver, 2013).

The evolution of PFI over time

How did PFI evolve over time and in different regions of the United Kingdom? Using an approach similar to Navarro-Espigares and Martín-Segura (2011), this section provides an overview of PFI at different levels of government, in different regions, and for different sectors.[1] Data come from HM Treasury's publicly available Excel spreadsheet containing current projects as of 31 March 2014 (HM Treasury, 2014a). Each project in the dataset is assigned to a level of government (i.e. central government, devolved authority (N. Ireland, Scotland, and Wales), local authority, or NHS) based on the procuring authority listed in the dataset.[2] Financial year is determined based on the date of financial close for each PFI project. Assignment of projects to regions and sectors is provided in the dataset.[3]

Data show that the volume of PFI projects grew over the course of the 1990s, reaching its highest levels between 1999 and 2007 (Figure 3.2.). While the earliest PFI projects were procured by the central government, by the 2000s, all levels of government were involved in PFI procurement, with local authorities' procurement representing a substantial portion of total capital value. As of March 2014, 728 PFI contracts were in operation or under construction with a total capital value of GBP 56.6 billion; an additional 11 projects were in procurement with an expected capital value of GBP 816.1 million (HM Treasury, 2014b). The value of deals peaked in 2007/08, with a value of GBP 8.4 billion signed in that year, but dropped off in the face of the financial crisis.

The financial crisis had a notable effect on the PFI programme. After 2008, the availability of finance for PFI projects narrowed, debt margins rose, and total private finance costs were only partially offset by declining interest rates (NAO, 2010). These rising costs raised questions about the value for money of PFI compared to traditional procurement (NAO, 2010).[4] Although some projects went forward, the number of new deals dropped dramatically (Figure 3.2.). According to Winch (2012: 118), "in July 2010, the new administration cancelled all 'Building Schools for the Future' projects that had not already reached financial close, on value for money grounds. Similarly, 7 of the 18 municipal waste PFI projects that had not yet reached financial close were cancelled in October 2010". In 2013/14, nine new projects were agreed to with a capital value of GBP 1.4 billion (Booth and Starodubtseva, 2015).

Figure 3.2. Evolution of the number and total capital value of current PFI projects by level of government

As of March 2014

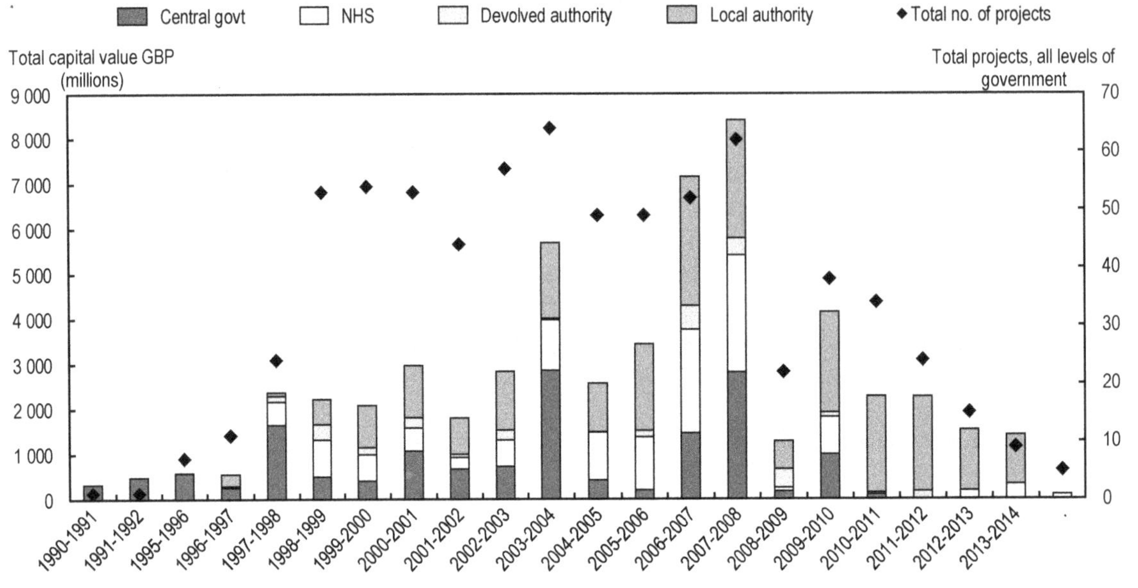

Note: Assignment to level of government is based on the "procuring authority" listed in the dataset. Current projects exclude expired or terminated projects and projects in procurement.

Source: Author's calculation based on HM Treasury (2014), "Current projects as at 31 March 2014", Excel.

The most valuable projects tend to be awarded by the central government. For current projects as of March 2014, both the maximum and the average value of central government projects tended to be much higher than other levels of government (Table 3.1). However, as Table 3.2 reveals, in terms of volume, most projects are procured by lower levels of government (60% of total projects are procured by local authorities; 7% by devolved authorities). Thus, while central government projects often have the highest capital value, devolved and local authorities represent nearly half of the total capital value procured as of March 2014. However, as will be shown later, although subnational governments procure a great deal of capital value, they are not solely responsible for paying for it. It is also worth noting that despite the increase in the number of deals in the 2000s, PFI/PPP projects accounted for approximately 10–15% of English local authority capital investment during the latter half of the decade (House of Lords, 2010).

Table 3.1. Capital value of current PFI projects by level of government, entire United Kingdom as of March 2014

Level of government	Capital value (GBP millions)				% of Total Capital Value
	Maximum Project Value	Average Project Value	Minimum Project Value	Total Capital Value	
Central government	2687.6	158.6	4.0	15,701	28%
NHS	1149.0	95.4	1.1	13,072	23%
Devolved authority	320.0	62.2	3.0	2,986	5%
Local authority	644.0	56.4	1.4	24,794	44%

Note: Assignment to level of government is based on the procuring authority. Current projects exclude expired or terminated projects and projects in procurement.
Source: Author's calculation based on HM Treasury (2014), "Current projects as at 31 March 2014", Excel.

Table 3.2. Number of current PFI projects by level of government, entire United Kingdom, as of March 2014

Level of government	Projects in construction	Projects in operation	Total number of projects	% of total projects
Central govt		101	101	14%
NHS	4	133	137	19%
Devolved authority		50	50	7%
Local authority	53	387	440	60%
Total	57	671	728	100%

Note: Assignment to level of government is based on the procuring authority. Current projects exclude expired or terminated projects and projects in procurement.
Source: Author's calculation based on HM Treasury (2014), "Current projects as at 31 March 2014", Excel.

As in Espigares and Martín-Segura (2011), the data reveal regional variation in PFI procurement across the UK (Figure 3.3.). London stands out as the region with the greatest number of projects and the highest accumulated capital value. However, once population is taken into account, the total capital value per inhabitant in London – while higher than other English regions – is no longer the highest in the UK. Northern Ireland and Scotland both stand out with higher per capita values. In Northern Ireland, the total value of projects is relatively low and procured largely by the devolved government. There are no PFI projects for which a local council is the procuring authority. In Scotland, the total value is the 4th highest of 12 regions, with procurement undertaken by all levels of government. Scottish local authorities represent a significant share of total projects and total value. Wales trails all other regions with low PFI penetration.

Figure 3.3. Total capital value of current PFI projects by region, level of government, and per capita value, entire United Kingdom as of March 2014

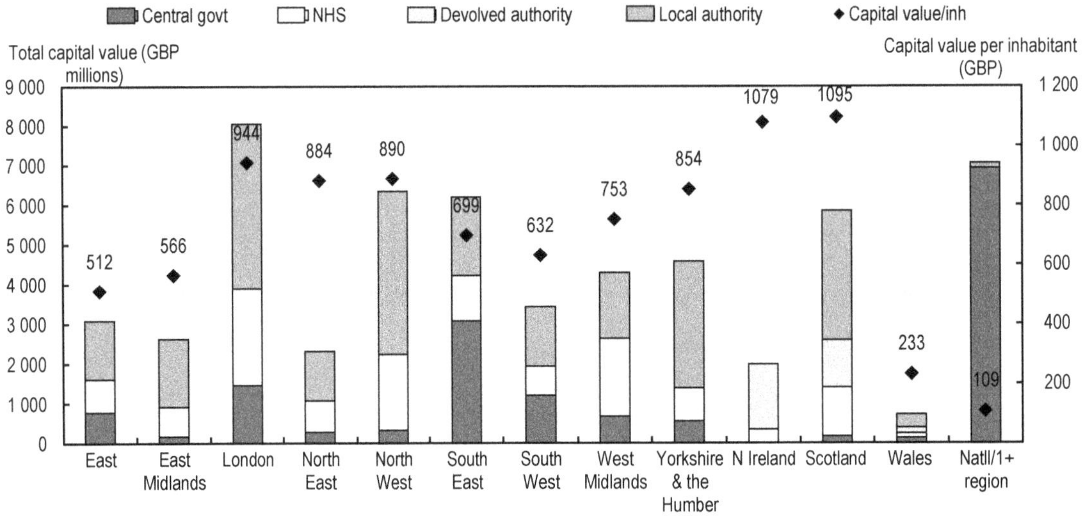

Note: Assignment to level of government is based on the procuring authority. The data already assign projects to regions. Current projects exclude expired or terminated projects and projects in procurement.
Source: Author's calculation based on HM Treasury (2014), "Current projects as at 31 March 2014", Excel; ONS (2015), "MYE2: Population Estimates by single year of age and sex for local authorities in the United Kingdom, mid-2014", Excel, version 25 June 2015.

Figure 3.4. Total number of current PFI projects by region and level of government, entire United Kingdom as of March 2014

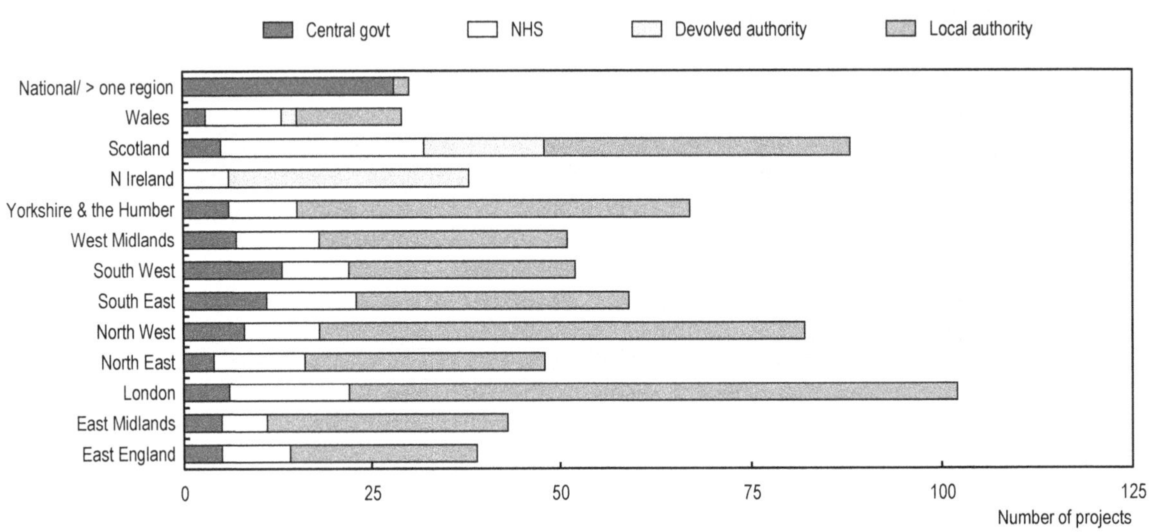

Note: Assignment to level of government is based on the procuring authority. The data already assign projects to regions. Current projects exclude expired or terminated projects and projects in procurement.
Source: Author's calculation based on HM Treasury (2014), "Current projects as at 31 March 2014", Excel.

Figure 3.5. . Total capital value and number of current PFI projects by sector and level of government, entire United Kingdom as of March 2014

A. Total capital value in GBP millions

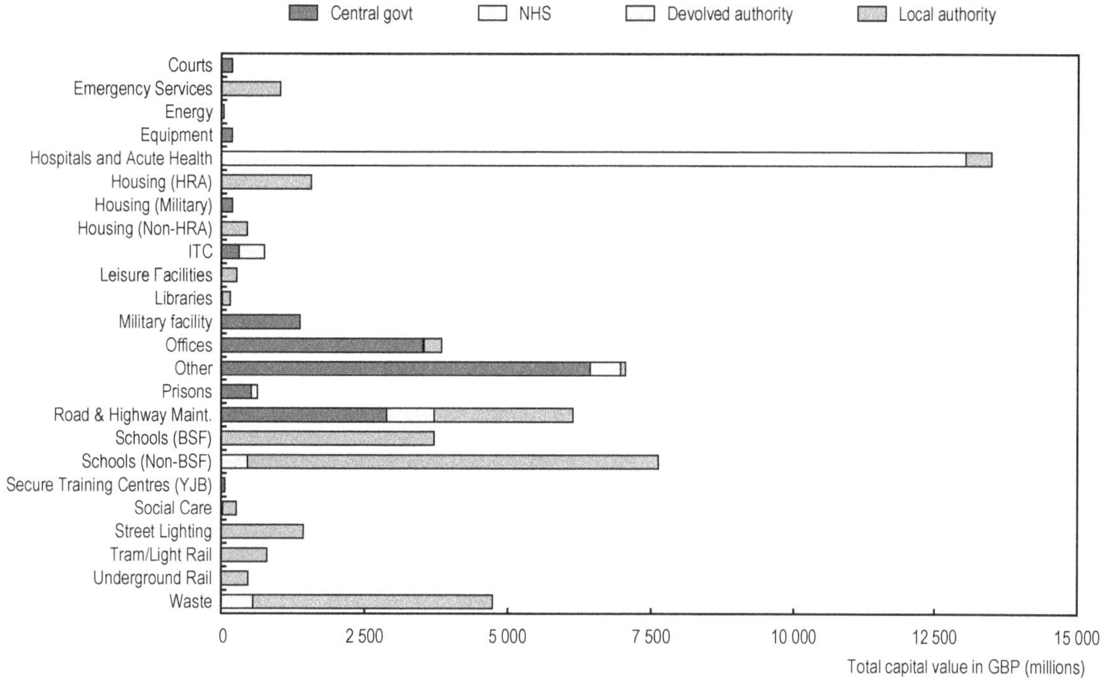

B. Number of current PFI projects

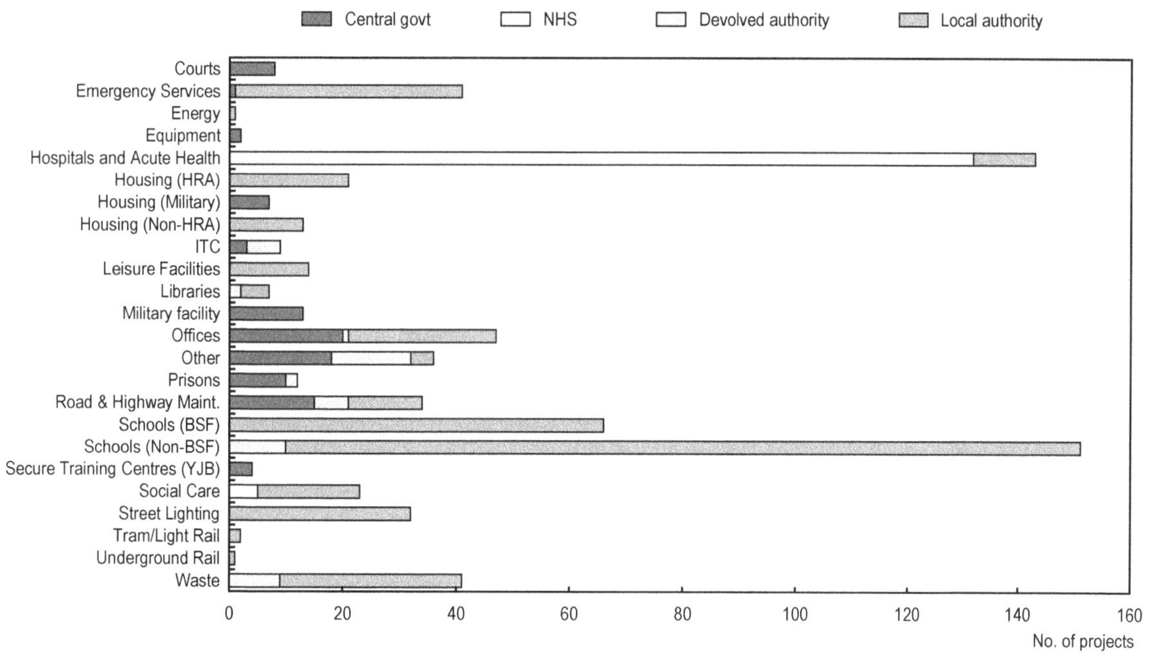

Note: Assignment to level of government is based on the procuring authority. Current projectsexclude expired or terminated projects and projects in procurement.

Source: Author's calculation based on HM Treasury (2014), "Current projects as at 31 March 2014", Excel.

PFI has traditionally been associated with social infrastructure such as health, education, and housing – although the model has been used for other infrastructure such as transportation. Examining PFIs by sector underscores the priority for social infrastructure. Since the early 1990s, the greatest total capital value has been generated in health and hospitals through projects procured largely through the National Health Service. Between 1990 and March 2014, a total of 143 health PFI projects were procured worth a total capital value of GBP 13.5 billion. Of these, 132 are attributed to NHS entities and the remainder to local governments. Although the greatest value was generated via health projects, education projects were, in fact, most numerous and rank second in terms of capital value. 217 PFI projects in education were procured both via the "Building Schools for the Future" (BSF) programme and otherwise. Their total capital value was GBP 11.3 billion for both categories combined. All school projects were subnational ones, with the overwhelming majority procured by local authorities. By contrast, transport projects – which also generated substantial value – were split between the central and local levels. Road and highway projects are shared between levels of government, while tram/light rail/underground rail were pursued as local projects. PFI has also been tapped for office space, street lighting, waste management, prisons, and emergency service projects.

Following the 2008 financial crisis, the central government's infrastructure focus shifted away from social infrastructure towards economic infrastructure (LexisPSL and Addleshaw Goddard, n.d.-b; NAO, 2011). This shift intended to reinforce global competitiveness and to create jobs (LexisPSL and Addleshaw Goddard, n.d.-b). Since 2010, these priorities have been articulated in the Government's National Infrastructure Plan (NIP), a long-term strategy for addressing infrastructure in key sectors through 2020 and beyond. The 2014 NIP contained information on planned public and private sector investment in infrastructure valued at over GBP 460 billion (approx. 25% of GDP) through 2020 and beyond (LexisPSL, n.d.; Pisu et al., 2015). Approximately two-thirds of the financing for the 550 projects and programmes in the NIP was expected to come from private sources, 21% from the public sector, and 14% from mixed (public-private) sources (Pisu et al., 2015). Thus, there is interest in attracting private capital, but the priority given to PFI/PF2 as a mechanism for delivering infrastructure appears diminished although it remains in use. The Priority Schools Building Programme to refurbish 260 schools, for example, uses PF2 (EFA, 2015; HM Treasury, 2014c).

Multi-level governance context

Subnational public private partnerships in the UK occur in a context of multi-level governance. The UK, as a highly centralised unitary country, exerts a great deal of influence over subnational governments, particularly in England. However, as responsibility for capital expenditures is devolved, there is some variation in approach across the UK. This section examines the various laws, regulations, policies, and actors associated with PPPs that exist at multiple levels of government, and the complexities and co-ordination challenges that emerge from such arrangements.

Actors

Numerous actors at different levels of government play a role in the implementation of public private partnerships for infrastructure delivery in the UK. In terms of contracting authorities for PFI/PF2, central government departments, devolved administrations (i.e. Scotland, Northern Ireland, and Wales), arms-length entities (e.g. NHS Trusts), and local authorities are all able to enter into PFI/PF2 contracts. It is important to clarify that the term "local authority" includes a variety of local bodies. In total there are 353 "principal local authorities" in England with statutory responsibility for public services (NAO, 2015a). These include "single-tier" bodies and "two tier" bodies (where responsibilities are shared between a county council and a district council). Strategic or combined authorities have also been created to carry out certain functions (e.g. the Greater London Authority) (NAO, 2015b). In Scotland, Wales, and Northern Ireland, all local authorities are "single-tier". There are 32 local authorities in Scotland, 22 in Wales, and 11 (previously 26) in Northern Ireland (Scottish Government, 2015; Welsh Government, 2015a; Northern Ireland Executive, 2015). Local competences are not the same everywhere. Local authorities' competences in Northern Ireland are more limited than elsewhere (CEMR, 2012; Northern Ireland Executive, 2015).

Regulatory and supporting authorities also exist at all levels of government. At the central government level, key actors are associated with HM Treasury. Various actors have been created within HM Treasury over the years to address infrastructure priorities and in some cases PPPs in particular.[5] Until recently, the primary central government actor was Infrastructure UK (IUK), established in 2009 to focus on England's long-term infrastructure priorities with a goal of facilitating private sector investment including PPPs (EPEC, 2012a). In 2010, it incorporated Partnerships UK (PUK), a PPP unit which was itself a PPP between HM Treasury and the private sector that operated for a number of years to promote and support PPP deals (discussed under administrative capacity) (EPEC, 2012a). In January 2016, IUK was replaced by the Infrastructure and Projects Authority, a merger of IUK with the Major Projects Authority, which oversaw the largest government projects (Cabinet Office, 2015). Also important at the central level are the line ministries (departments), which play a role in local PFI projects in England. This is true for the Department for Communities and Local Government, for example, with respect to housing (OECD, 2015). The role of the Department for Environment, Food and Rural Affairs (Defra) in local waste PFI projects is discussed later.

With limited exception, responsibility for infrastructure and public private partnerships is devolved to Scotland, Wales and Northern Ireland (LexisPSL and Addleshaw Goddard, n.d.-c). In Scotland, infrastructure projects are administered by the Infrastructure Investment Unit, which is part of the Finance Directorate (EPEC, 2012c). Its responsibilities include sponsorship of the Scottish Futures Trust (SFT) established in 2008 to seek best value in infrastructure investment (including but not limited to PPPs) across the region (EPEC, 2012c). SFT provides assistance to the Scottish government, health boards, and local authorities to structure and implement PPPs. In Wales, the Infrastructure Investment Plan is the Welsh Assembly's primary vehicle to prioritise and deliver capital investment (Welsh Government, 2015b; LexisPSL and Addleshaw Goddard, n.d.-c). In Northern Ireland, infrastructure planning and delivery are the responsibility of the Strategic Investment Board, an advisory company owned by and accountable to the Office of the First Minister and deputy First Minister (OFMDFM) (EPEC, 2012b). Other key players include the Central Finance Unit in the Department of Finance and Personnel, the Economic Policy Unit, and the Public Private Investment Unit in the OFMDFM (EPEC, 2012b).

Finally, at the local level, (as noted previously) local authorities have responsibility for procuring and managing PPP and PFI projects. In Northern Ireland, local authorities have played little role to date in PFI projects (EPEC, 2012b). In England, local authorities' capacity to design and deliver projects (and renegotiate contracts) is supported by Local Partnerships, a joint venture between the Local Government Association and HM Treasury. Some local authorities, such as Leeds, have also developed their own "PPP unit", to reinforce capacity for PFI projects (Partnerships Bulletin, 2007; EPEC, 2012a). It is worth noting that although local authorities frequently act as the procuring authority for PFI contracts, the projects involved are often part of central government programmes (NAO, 2009a). As such, they contribute toward national goals, are often (partially) financed via central government funds (NAO, 2011), and regulated by central government guidance.

Legal and regulatory arrangements

Regulatory coherence across levels of government with respect to PPPs poses relatively few issues in England. There is no specific "PPP law" but "there is sufficient flexibility and certainty within the statutory and common law framework to recognise and permit PPPs" (EPEC, 2012a: 23). As a unitary country, local authorities are very much subject to centrally promulgated regulations, with some variation across regions and little variation across local authorities. HM Treasury heavily influences PFI/PF2 contract provisions for all levels of government in England and Wales, and somewhat less so for Northern Ireland and Scotland. When drafting PFI contracts, English and Welsh public authorities – including local governments – must use standardized guidance referred to as "Standardisation of PFI Contracts (SoPC)" (see discussion in the section regarding administrative capacity). Contract models for Northern Ireland and Scotland are generally consistent with or reflect the SoPC (EPEC, 2012b; 2012c).

Regulatory influence also exists at the supra-national level. Authorities at all levels of government have had to abide by EU procurement law, the main aspects of which can be found in the Public Contracts Directive (2014/24/EU), the Utilities Contracts Directive (2014/25/EU) and the Concessions Directive (2014/23/EU) (LexisPSL and Digings, n.d.).[6] According to LexisPSL and Addleshaw Goddard (n.d.-c), "in addition … the principles of the Treaty on European Union (including transparency, proportionality, equal treatment and mutual recognition) must be considered when a public body awards contracts for certain works or services to a third party." Supranational influence has also been felt when the national government relies on local authorities to achieve compliance with EU directives. This is the case, for example, with the 1999 European Union Landfill Directive (1999/31/EC) and the "Waste Infrastructure Delivery Programme" (WIDP) discussed in Section 4.

Of particular importance to the PPP landscape has been the influence of statistical treatment of PPPs. These rules, embodied in the European System of Integrated Economic Accounts (ESA), determine how infrastructure projects are classified with respect to debt and deficit figures in National Accounts. PFI contracts recorded in the National Accounts also feed into the calculation of Public Sector Net Debt (Booth and Starodubtseva, 2015) which has been associated with fiscal rules (House of Commons, 2011). Until recently, statistical treatment of PPPs was undertaken in the basis of ESA95. Depending largely on risk allocation, PPP projects are classified as either on or off the national government's balance sheet (EPEC, 2010). Where the majority of risk is borne by the private sector, the project is "off balance sheet." By contrast, "on balance sheet" projects count toward a national government's public debt and annual budget deficit limits under the Excessive Deficit Procedure (EDP) under the Maastricht Treaty (60% of GDP and 3% of GDP, respectively) (EPEC, 2010). Revised rules were implemented under ESA10 in September 2014 (EPEC, 2015) with greater emphasis placed not only risk allocation but also control of the project. Although the UK is not subject to sanctions under the EDP (EC, 2015), in general the Eurostat rules produce an incentive to consider (and possibly alter) PPP structures depending on the impact on National Accounts (EPEC, 2010). These incentives likely flow to the local level.

Complicating matters is a divergence between statistical treatment of PFI/PPP projects (i.e. ESA95/ESA10) and accounting treatment of the same projects. Accounting treatment of PPPs is set at the national level (EPEC, 2010). Until 2009, public authorities employed UK GAAP (Generally Accepted Accounting Practice) rules to define whether or not PFI projects were to appear on or off their balance sheets. The UK GAAP criteria and ESA95 criteria produced similar results with respect to PFI, and thus public authorities' financial accounts and National Accounts did not conflict (House of Lords, 2010). In 2009, however, the UK switched to the International Financial Reporting Standards (IFRS) and under this regime many PFI projects moved on-balance sheet, leading to a discrepancy between accounting treatment and statistical treatment of PPPs (House of Lords, 2010). For the UK, the solution has been the separate reporting of the statistical treatment (under ESA95/ESA10) and accounting treatment (under IFRS) of PFI projects (EPEC, 2010). According to UK NAO (2011:8), "although there is well developed Treasury guidance on assessing value for money of PFI projects, the method of calculating public sector net debt may, even though the financial accounting treatment has changed, continue to act as an incentive to use PFI as it often leaves liabilities off the national balance sheet."

Beginning in 2011 the UK government introduced the annual publication of the Whole of Government Accounts (WGA). According to HM Treasury (2012), the WGA are full accruals based accounts covering the public sector. It consolidates the accounts of about 1500 bodies at all levels of government, including the health service and public corporations. The WGA categorizes PPPs according to IFRS (and thus largely on the balance sheet). It provides a publicly available summary of the long-term contractual commitments and contingent liabilities associated with PFI (or similar) projects (HM Treasury, 2012; OECD, 2015). According to the OECD (2015:8), "despite the WGA there can still be an accounting incentive to use PFI, but this is now minimal and stems mainly from compliance with [ESA] rules."

Financing and funding

Before discussing financing of PFI projects, it is worth asking: Why would local authorities consider PFI at all? While the prospect of efficiency gains and better coverage of asset maintenance may well have played an important role increasing the appeal of PFI, a major driver behind its uptake at the local level is likely to have been the "desire for additionality to the public funding capability" (Winch et al., 2012: 5). Local government capital budgets had been under pressure from the central government for some time at the outset of the Private Finance Initiative (Wilson and Game, 2011). According to these authors, until 2004 the central government maintained tight control over three sources of local capital financing: local borrowing, capital receipts, and capital grants. It was not until the introduction of the prudential borrowing regime in 2004 that local authorities could realistically consider financing substantial capital expenditure themselves. Capital grants were available from the central government, but until recently they were largely earmarked (Wilson and Game, 2011). In addition, UK fiscal targets regarding its Public Sector Net Debt (PSND) as a percentage of GDP (ONS, 2006; OECD, 2009) between 1997 and 2008, as well as the EU Maastricht targets (ONS, 2006), likely discouraged public authorities at all levels from accumulating capital projects on their balance sheets.[7] In short, PFI promised additionality.

The additionality of PFI comes from the fact that expenditures from capital budgets that would have to be made in the present under traditional procurement are substituted for payments from current expenditure budgets in the future. A PFI project traditionally involves establishing a Special Purpose Vehicle (SPV) to raise capital for infrastructure development in which the project is financed via private sector equity and debt. The SPV is later repaid via fixed government payments over the life of the project, beginning in the operational phase (called "unitary charges"). "Unitary charges include payments for ongoing services (e.g. maintenance, cleaning, catering and security) associated with these projects, as well as repayment of and interest on debt used to finance the capital costs" (HM Treasury, 2014b: 11). Payments are made from revenue (current) spending.

There are pros and cons associated with unitary charges. On the positive side, because the annual unitary payments are long-term contractual obligations, they are predictable and offer substantial price certainty (Corner, 2006). Moreover, contractors have an incentive to deliver projects on-time because the payments generally do not start until the asset is operational (Corner, 2006). Finally, because unitary payments are to cover whole life costs, the contractor has an incentive to seek efficiencies over the life of the contract (Corner, 2006).

There are also downsides of unitary charge payments. First, because PFI project financing relies (in large part) on debt issued at commercial rates that tend to be higher than government borrowing rates, taxpayers generally pay higher borrowing costs via PFI than they would have under traditional procurement (Corner, 2006). Second, unitary charge payments extend for many years and "constitute one of the first claims on local authority budgets" (Cuthbert and Cuthbert, 2011). As discussed later, historically local government unitary payments have been partially subsidized by the central government with the remaining portion coming from own revenues. In the UK, local authorities have very little own revenue at their disposal. As a result, local governments face limited room for manoeuvre when obliged to make set unitary charge payments while also trimming budgets. This means in times of fiscal constraint, "other parts of local authority services … have to bear the brunt of budget cuts" (Cuthbert and Cuthbert, 2011). In their examination of PFI schools projects in Scotland, Cuthbert and Cuthbert (2011), find that this situation is exacerbated where local contributions to unitary charges have been indexed at a rate that exceeds inflation and by poor affordability assessments on the part of local authorities. They hold local authorities accountable for failing to adequately implement Treasury guidance, and higher levels of government accountable for poor oversight. In England, inflation on unitary charge payments has outpaced that of revenues. Many local governments are thus confronting affordability issues on their PFI projects.

As Figure 3.6. indicates, since the launch of PFI in 1992 through 2050, unitary charge payments attributable to local government constitute a sizeable proportion of total unitary charges. Total PFI unitary charge payments for 2015-16 were expected to amount to GBP 10.5 billion, with approximately GBP 3.7 billion attributable to local authorities. On a per capita basis, local authority unitary charges appear greatest for North West England and Scotland, and smallest in Wales. Since the reform of PFI in 2012, central and subnational governments have sought to identify and recoup savings via PFI contract reviews and renegotiations. Local Partnerships, for example, has worked with over 57 public sector organisations, including local authorities, to identify around GBP 1.2 billion in PFI contract savings (Local Partnerships, 2016) (nominal whole life cost). This includes, for example, a savings of GBP 4.1 million over the life of a PFI street lighting contract for Newcastle and North Tyneside which originally had unitary charges totalling GBP 74.8 million (nominal whole life cost) (Local Partnerships, n.d).

Figure 3.6. Nominal unitary charge payments by level of government through 2050/51

(For current projects, as of 31 March 2014)

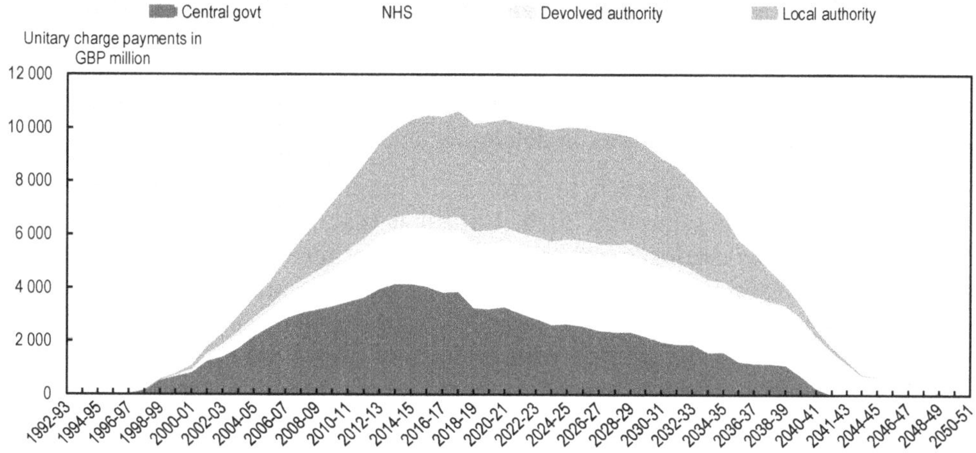

Note: Assignment to level of government is based on the procuring authority. Current projects exclude expired or terminated projects and projects in procurement. Unitary charges in nominal terms, not discounted.
Source: Author's calculation based on HM Treasury (2014), "Current projects as at 31 March 2014", Excel.

Figure 3.7. Local authority unitary charges per capita by region, 1997/98 through 2037

(For current projects, as of 31 March 2014)

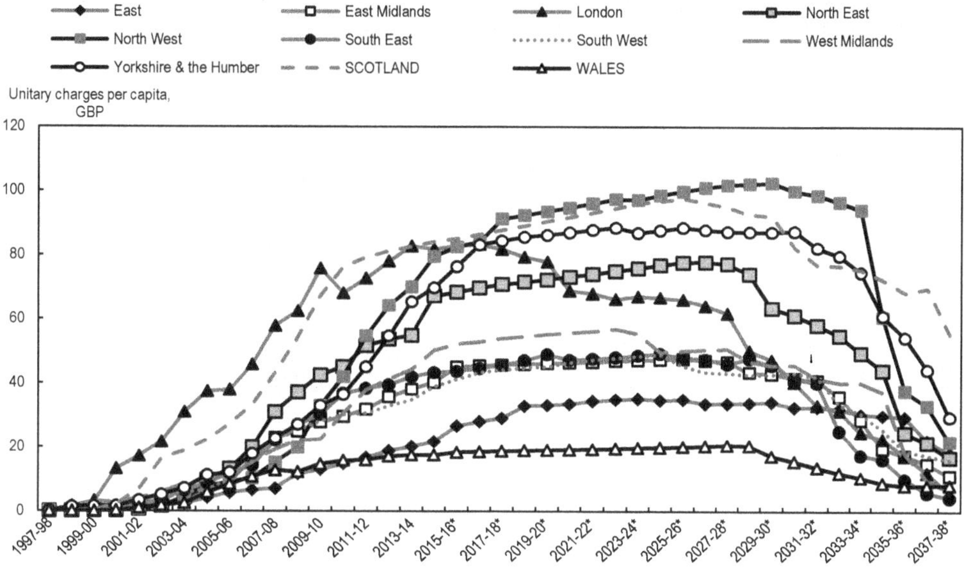

Note: Unitary charges per capita are estimated by aggregating local authorities' projects' unitary charges to the regional level on an annual basis and dividing the sum by population values and projections available through 2037. Unitary charges extend past this date, but population projections were not available at the time of calculation. Figures are nominal, not discounted. Assignment of PFI projects to the local level was done on the basis of procuring authority. There are no projects for N. Ireland in which the procuring authority was a local government. Current projects exclude expired or terminated projects and projects in procurement.
Source: Author's calculation based on HM Treasury (2014), "Current projects as at 31 March 2014", Excel; ONS, "Table 1: 2012-based Subnational Population Projections for Regions in England", 29 May 2014, Excel; StatsWales, "2012-based national population projections for Wales, 2012-2037", Excel; National Records of Scotland, "Population Projections for Scottish Areas (2012-based)", Excel; OECD, UK regional population statistics (TL2) 1992-2012, Excel, extracted from OECD.stat 12 Oct 2015.

Local authorities are not the only entities facing trade-offs between services and making unitary charge payments. NHS trusts have received much attention for their fiscal distress associated with PFI payments. For example, Peterborough and Stamford NHS Trust is "one of seven trusts with unaffordable PFI debts to receive money from a special GBP 1.5bn Department of Health (DoH) bailout fund to help keep them afloat" (Campbell, 2012). Unitary charges also present potential downsides to the private sector which can face unexpected delays, costs, and losses in delivering a project.

Incentives for a PFI-led approach to local asset development were likely enhanced by central government policy through 2010. Until that year, the central government offered "PFI credits" for English local authorities wishing to pursue PFI projects. The credits, issued through central government departments, were grants made available to local authorities to assist with repaying the capital investment (via unitary charges) once a PFI project was operational. The grants/credits effectively subsidized unitary charge payments. To access PFI credits, projects needed to meet specific conditions including compliance with SoPC guidance and a requirement that the project be off-balance sheet (EPEC, 2012a; NAO, 2009a). PFI projects that were off the local authority's balance sheet under UK GAAP rules (and thus ESA95) did not count against the central department's capital expenditure budget. By contrast, on-budget projects did. The NAO (2009a: 39) reported that "allocating each Department a set amount of PFI credits each year provides an incentive for the Department to pursue off-balance sheet projects. PFI credits are used by Departments as if they were another capital budget in addition to [their capital department expenditure limit], solely for off-balance sheet projects." This approach could also provide an incentive for local authorities to structure projects to be off-budget and capture PFI credits rather than necessarily maximize value-for-money.[8]

As of February 2010, different central government departments had committed GBP 22 billion in PFI credits to 364 projects, with an additional GBP 7.3 billion in credits for 73 projects in the pipeline (Table 3.3). The credits were abandoned in 2010 as they were seen to distort the assessment of whether or not PFI was the appropriate procurement method and, in doing so, create a bias toward PFI (HM Treasury, 2012). Some of the credits were later retracted for budgetary reasons, as in the case of the waste infrastructure that follows. Similar subsidies were provided by the Scottish government in the form of "level playing field support". These funds provided by the Scottish Executive to local authorities via the General Revenue Grant were to assist them with unitary charge payments associated with PFI projects (Cuthbert and Cuthbert, 2011). The level playing field support continues as grants to local governments (see Box 3.2 on private finance in Scotland).

Table 3.3. Value of PFI credits for English Local Authority projects

(GBP million, through February 2010)

Sponsoring Department	Pipeline	Endorsed	Signed	Operational	Ended	Total
Dept. for Children, Schools and Families (DCSF)	3,060	3,739	1,421	5,512	30	13,762
Department for Transport (DfT)	1,069	2,517	299	1,150		5,035
Dept. for Communities and Local Government (CLG) Housing	1,928	1,106	37	1,303		4,374
Dept. for Communities and Local Government (CLG) Fire	123	214	42	176		555
Dept. for Communities and Local Government (CLG) Other		81	80	270	20	450
Department for Environment, Food & Rural Affairs (DEFRA)	258	1,695		890		2,844
Home Office (HO)	655	186		519		1,360
Department of Health (DH)	268	93		256		616
Department for Culture, Media & Sport (DCMS)		93	79	207		379
Total (Value)	**7,360**	**9,723**	**1,959**	**10,283**	**49**	**29,374**
Total (Number)	**73**	**79**	**25**	**255**	**5**	**437**

Note: According to notes accompanying the data, the PFI credit value of "pipeline" projects is provisional and can change when the project is "endorsed" and ready to enter the procurement process. The credit value of "endorsed" projects may change during the procurement process, but is more stable than pipeline projects.

Source: DCLG (2010), "Local Authority PFI Projects, as of Feb 2010, Excel.

Economies of scale

Because PFI focused on social infrastructure, most PFI projects (even bundled ones like schools) have tended to stay within administrative boundaries. Local PFIs have tended to correspond to local competences that do not have significant cross-border co-ordination requirements, such as schools. An exception may be waste management. Yet small-scale projects that may appeal to local governments are not always appropriate for the PFI approach. They do not necessarily represent value for money nor are they commercially viable (Vernon and Sanders, 2007). The UK's standardised PFI guidance (SoPC4, discussed below) explicitly indicated that "the PFI is not suitable for projects with a capital value of less than GBP 20 million" (HM Treasury, 2007: 3). Efforts were made to create alternatives to a traditional PFI contract to tap the benefits of the PPP approach, put forward commercially viable projects, and achieve economies of scale (Vernon and Sanders, 2007). These either incorporated the use of PFI or involved alternative procurement. The approaches have included strategic partnering, multi-authority procurement, and multi-service projects (Vernon and Sanders, 2007):

- **Strategic partnering** models have included the *Local Improvement Finance Trust (LIFT)* scheme for aggregating smaller health projects into larger schemes undertaken via joint venture involving the central government (Partnerships for Health), the local health body, and a private partner. A similar model was put in place for schools. The *Building Schools for the Future (BSF)* programme similarly involved aggregating school projects via a joint venture (a Local Education Partnership), that brought together the central government (Partnerships for Schools), the local authority and a private partner to develop and deliver school projects via private finance (PFI) or traditional design-build contracts (Vernon and Sanders, 2007);
- At the local level, **multi-authority procurement** has involved different local authorities either jointly procuring an asset and separately contracting for services,

or jointly procuring both the asset and services. Such joint procurement was encouraged by the central government and by the local government association as a way to increase procurement efficiency. It was encouraged for waste sector PFIs seeking to secure PFI credits (Vernon and Sanders, 2007); and

- Finally, **multi-service projects** bring together a variety of services under one roof (i.e. a one-stop shop). Commonly referred to as a Joint Service Centre, these projects were commonly procured via PFI or LIFT schemes (Vernon and Sanders, 2007).

Seeking efficiency gains through joint procurement has not been restricted to England. In Scotland, the "hub" model brings together multiple public authorities in a geographic area and is a potential facilitator of collaboration. This is encouraged by the Scottish government, particularly for small-scale projects (see Box 3.2). Despite some evidence of joint procurement and shared assets, such collaboration is underutilised for public investment generally (Audit Scotland, 2013) and possibly for PPPs. At least in Scotland, local authorities report challenges aligning timetables and priorities (Audit Scotland, 2013).

Administrative capacity

Public private partnership arrangements are well-documented as complex transactions requiring expertise in a variety of areas. A lack of sufficient capacity for these complex transactions has been noted at the central and local levels alike (NAO, 2011). While both levels of government can face capacity challenges, the problems for local authorities can be more acute. From the outset of the PFI programme, the UK has actively worked to build and reinforce public sector capacity to engage effectively with the private sector. Its primary strategy has been to establish PPP units and other institutional structures to strengthen government capacity, reinforce project scrutiny, and provide financial resources to local governments to access technical support.[9]

With respect to institutional support, until 2010 the UK had three units at the national level working on PPPs: Partnerships UK (PUK), HM Treasury's PPP Policy Team, and HM Treasury's Infrastructure Finance Unit. In 2010, the three entities were consolidated and replaced by Infrastructure UK (Istrate and Puentes, 2011). PUK was active during the main years of growth of the PFI programme (2000-2010).[10] It was a fee-charging, public-private entity that worked with public authorities at all levels of government to facilitate PPP/PFI transactions and, to a lesser extent, support operational PPPs (EPEC, 2012a; PUK, 2009). IUK, by contrast, is wholly government owned. In addition to support from the national level, direct assistance is available to English local authorities via Local Partnerships (LP). LP is a joint venture between the Local Government Association and HM Treasury. It is the successor to 4ps (the Public Private Partnerships Programme) established in 1996 by the English and Welsh local government associations to help extent the PFI model to the local level (4ps, 2009; Winch, 2012). It supports local authorities' capacity for procurement, project management, contract management, and funding and partnering abilities. Services have included independent scrutiny of PPP projects at key stages (gateway reviews) (EPEC, 2012a).

Reinforced scrutiny of local government projects came largely through the Project Review Group (PRG). The PRG, which involved representation from HM Treasury, the ministry responsible for local government (DCLG), and 4ps, oversaw the approval process of local projects receiving PFI credits (EPEC, 2012a) and was deemed "valuable" for project assurance (NAO, 2011: 7). Despite this, the NAO (2011: 7) pointed to scope for "greater project assurance." With the abolition of PFI credits in 2010, the PRG mechanism was dropped and scrutiny of local projects was merged into the central government's approval process for major projects (EPEC, 2012a). Local projects which receive no central government funding are not subject to this process and "have no formal interaction with central government" (EPEC, 2012a: 26).

Finally, the use of standardized contract documents helped to attenuate some of the risks presented by the complexity of PPP contracts and administrative capacity constraints of the public sector. The Standardisation of PFI Contracts (SoPC), developed by PUK and HM Treasury in 1999, provided standardized guidelines for PFIs. Updated four times through 2007, the last version (SoPC4) was succeeded by PF2 guidance. The use of SoPC aimed "first, to promote a common understanding of the main risks which are encountered in a standard PFI project; secondly, to allow consistency of approach and pricing across a range of similar projects; and thirdly, to reduce the time and costs of negotiation by enabling all parties concerned to agree a range of areas that can follow a standard approach without extended negotiation" (HM Treasury, 2007: 1). Use of SoPC, or approved sector-specific contracts such as for health and education, has been mandatory in England and Wales (HM Treasury, 2007; EPEC, 2012a) but models in Scotland and Ireland have been consistent with the SoPC (EPEC, 2012b; 2012c). There is some scope for procuring authorities to tailor individual contracts to meet project needs but any changes are subject to approval by HM Treasury (OECD, 2015). Consideration for local authority contracts above and beyond the SoPC4 were issued by 4ps in its "Local Authority Supplement to SoPC" (HM Treasury, 2007). The use of the SoPC and the limitation on alternatives has led to relatively uniform PFI contracts in England (EPEC, 2012a) and likely reinforced a minimum level of local capacity.

Much of the attention to public sector capacity appears to have revolved around project appraisal and effective procurement. Yet, because most PFI contracts have a life in excess of two decades, contract management is a critical but often underdeveloped public sector capacity. According to PWC (2011: 3), "PFIs rely upon the private sector regulating its own performance but this self-monitoring must be managed and tested as part of the public sector contract management function." Unfortunately, contract management teams are often "woefully under-resourced and contract managers are often unaware of their rights under the contract or how to enforce them" (pg. 2). The authors highlight the need to provide the same level of resources and support to contract managers as is provided to procurement teams.

Box 3.2. Private finance for infrastructure in Scotland

Scotland has substantial experience with various models of PPPs. From the late 1990s through 2010, the PFI approach to PPPs played an important role in infrastructure delivery. More recently, the Scottish government has emphasised new PPP models such as its non-profit distributing model (NPD) and hub models for infrastructure development. The motivations to pursue PFI (or PPPs more generally) have come, in part, from borrowing constraints. Until April 2015 (SFT, 2015a), the Scottish Government was unable to borrow to finance capital expenditures. Instead, traditionally procured capital expenditures had to be financed from the capital transfers received from the UK central government. PPPs (including PFI) offered additional resources for infrastructure investment, as well as the efficiency gains and long-term commitment to asset maintenance that come from the whole-of-life approach. In 2010, the UK spending review resulted in a 38% cut in capital transfers for Scotland (BBC, 2010), creating further impetus to seek private finance to meet infrastructure needs. Local authorities in Scotland can and do borrow for capital expenditure, but supplement this with capital transfers from the Scottish government and PPPs (i.e. PFI and NPD described below) (EPEC, 2012).

Responsibility for many areas of infrastructure and public private partnerships (exceptions include defence, telecoms, power) is devolved to Scotland, Wales and Northern Ireland. In Scotland, overall infrastructure investment is undertaken in the context of the "Infrastructure Investment Plan". The 2011 Plan sets out investment priorities and mechanisms to finance those investments through 2020. Infrastructure projects are administered by the Infrastructure Investment Unit within the Finance Directorate (LexisPSL and Addleshaw Goddard, n.d.). It sponsors the Scottish Futures Trust (SFT), set up in 2008 to help ensure value-for-money in infrastructure investment for the region, including but not limited to PPPs (EPEC, 2012).Between 1999 and 2010, PFI played an important role in infrastructure development. Although PPP policy and guidance is determined by the Scottish Government, during this period the approach to PPPs generally followed the Standardisation of PFI Contracts (SOPC) promulgated by HM Treasury (EPEC, 2012). According to 2014 HM Treasury data, over the period of 1999-00 to 2013-14, a total of 88 PFI projects for Scotland were signed with a capital value of GBP 5.85 billion. These data indicate that the UK government acted as the procuring authority for 5 projects, Scottish government (including Scottish Water) for 16, health bodies for 27, and local authorities for 40 projects. Local authority projects accounted for 56% of total capital value. Nearly all of this value is associated with school projects (Audit Scotland, 2013).

In 2010, concerns about PFI and particularly excessive private sector profits led the Scottish Government to develop an alternative, albeit similar, PPP model. The Non-Profit Distributing Model (NPD) is similar to PFI in many ways but distinguished by the fact that there is no dividend-bearing equity, private sector returns are capped, surpluses are distributed back to the public sector, and there is a public interest director to protect public sector interests. In contrast to PFI (but not PF2), soft services are also not included in the contract. NPD has to date been used for developing infrastructure in further education, transportation, and health (SFT, 2015b). The Scottish government set aside GBP 3.5 billion for the NPD programme and, as of March 2015, had GBP 1.8 billion of projects under construction (SFT, 2015b). Under the Hub model, public authorities in one of five designated geographical areas along with the Scottish Government (via SFT) enter into a joint venture with a private actor (a "hubco" company not unlike an SPV) to deliver a pipeline of infrastructure projects for the particular area. Projects delivered via the hubco can be traditionally procured, or procured via private finance. In the latter case, returns are capped. The Hub model is generally used for smaller projects than NPD. GBP 450 million of the GBP 1.25 billion "Scotland's Schools for the Future" programme is expected to be delivered via "hub" (EPEC, 2012). SFT also uses other models for facilitating private participation in (local) infrastructure, including the National Housing Trust and Tax Incremental Financing (EPEC, 2012). SFT provides technical support to procuring authorities for the different models.

Challenges to implementing PPP projects in Scotland are similar in many ways to those experienced in England. With respect to multi-level governance, while "value-for-money" is ostensibly the primary driver when it comes to choosing between traditional procurement or private finance, EU-driven classification treatment appears to play an important role in Scotland (as elsewhere in the UK). NPD and Hub projects that did not count toward public sector debt and deficit figures under ESA95 rules may be more likely to do so under new rules which came into effect in late 2014 (ESA10) (Dockreay, 2015). If this were to be the case, instead of providing the additionality needed to meet infrastructure needs, the projects could be counted against government capital budgets. The UK Office of National Statistics ruled that Scotland's largest NPD project, the Aberdeen Western Peripheral Route (AWPR), must be reclassified as public sector (Dockreay, 2015). In response, Scotland is expected to amend the AWPR contract and consider adjustments to the hub model in response to the new ESA10 rules (Dockreay, 2015).

With respect to financing and funding, it is important to note that while PFI has played an important role in infrastructure development, at the local level the amount of capital value procured via private finance was dwarfed by local capital expenditures. As of March 2013, local authorities had invested GBP 27 billion in infrastructure in real terms since 2000/01: GBP 23 billion from their capital budgets and nearly GBP 4 billion via private finance (PFI and NPD) (Audit Scotland, 2013). For PFI projects only (i.e. excluding NPD), unitary charges total GBP 31.3 billion through 2041-42, of which GBP 15.2 billion are associated with local authority projects (HM Treasury, 2014). Including both NPD and PFI payments, unitary charges for local authorities will peak in 2025/26 at approximately GBP 591 million (Audit Scotland, 2013). Local authorities only pay a portion of this cost, however. As with the English "PFI credits", the Scottish Government has traditionally provided funds to assist local authorities with unitary charges (previously called "level playing field support"). In 2012/13, this support amounted to 49% of the annual cost of the payments (Audit Scotland, 2013).

With respect to cross-jurisdictional co-ordination for PPPs, the hub model has the potential to facilitate collaboration. It is unique in that it combines entities across sectors (i.e. health, education, fire, police) in a given place and brings them together with a private development partner. While collaboration is not obligatory, it is encouraged by the Scottish government – particularly for projects that are too small to justify the overhead costs involved with launching a PPP. Despite all this, there are still challenges in getting different authorities to align priorities, budgets, and trust to make collaboration happen both for PPPs and for public investment generally (Audit Scotland, 2013).

As elsewhere, local administrative capacities in Scotland are mixed. There are 32 local authorities, many of which conduct very few PPPs. As a result, the in-house technical capacity to procure a complex PPP project may not necessarily exist. Even if it does, due to the infrequency of deals, it may not remain into the future. Once projects are closed, the contract monitoring is also a challenge. There can be a lack of understanding of the contract and how to ensure a contractor is delivering properly. As a result, local authorities may end up receiving less than expected from a PPP deal. Scottish Futures Trust (SFT) aims to reinforce local capacity by facilitating a transfer of resources, in the form of seconded staff, either from SFT to public authorities or among authorities themselves. They also carry out independent expert reviews at key stages of a project ("Gateway Reviews") to reinforce project planning and make adjustments if needed.

The 2013 Audit Scotland report on major capital projects at the local level suggests that good practices such as design quality assessment and gateway reviews are more likely to occur for PFI projects than traditionally procured ones.

Sources: Audit Scotland (2013), "Major capital investment in councils", Edinburgh; European PPP Expertise Centre (EPEC) (2012), "United Kingdom - Scotland: PPP Units and Related Institutional Framework", June 2012; LexisPSL and Addleshaw Goddard (n.d.), "UK infrastructure projects--relevant sources, government bodies and guidance", LexisPSL Practice Note; Scottish Futures Trust (SFT) (2015a), "SFTinvest", webpage, www.scottishfuturestrust.org.uk/our-work/funding-and-finance (accessed 7 Dec 2015); Scottish Futures Trust (SFT) (2015b), "Non-Profit Distributing (NPD)",webpage,www.scottishfuturestrust.org.uk/our-work/funding-and-finance/non-profit-distributing/ (accessed 3 Dec 2015); Dockreay, A. (2015), "ESA10: EU accounting trouble for Scotland's NPD scheme", IJGlobal, 6 Aug 2015; "Reforming PFI: Lessons from Scotland", SocInvest, 10 Oct 2012; HM Treasury (2014), "Current projects as at 31 March 2014", Excel; "Spending Review: Cuts 'threaten 12,000 Scottish jobs'", 20 Oct 2010, BBC News.

PFIs and England's "Waste Infrastructure Delivery Programme" (WIDP)

How have some of the issues raised in previous section played out with respect to specific PPPs? Some of the issues can be illustrated by examining England's "Waste Infrastructure Delivery Programme" (WIDP).

In 1999, the European Union issued the Landfill Directive (1999/31/EC) which set targets for member states to reduce the amount of biodegradable waste sent to landfills. Failure to meet targets can lead to fines (NAO, 2009b). Targets exist for England, Scotland, Northern Ireland and Wales (NAO, 2014). The UK's Department for Environment, Food and Rural Affairs (Defra) is responsible for ensuring that England achieves its targets (NAO, 2014). Prior to 2001, this responsibility lay with Defra's predecessor, the Department for the Environment, Transport and the Regions (NAO, 2014). It is local authorities, however, that are responsible for municipal waste disposal. The national strategy for achieving the EU targets thus heavily implies local authorities. They decide if and how to invest in waste disposal infrastructure (NAO, 2009b).

Despite the reliance on local authorities to achieve EU targets, prior to 2003 Defra did not have a clear strategy for facilitating new local waste infrastructure (NAO, 2009b). Moreover, intergovernmental relations were not particularly well organized to tap PFI as a mechanism for developing waste infrastructure capacity. According to the NAO (2009b), responsibility for managing the programme within the Department was unclear; early guidance for the PFI projects did not focus on landfill diversion or the EU directive; and the Department approved projects on a first-come, first-served basis. In 2006, Defra established the "Waste Infrastructure Delivery Programme" (WIDP) to "accelerate" development of local waste infrastructure by providing support and funding for waste PFI projects (NAO, 2014). The programme was given a clear structure, bringing together ~30 staff from Defra, Partnerships UK, and 4ps in a single team managed by Defra. Local authorities were invited to develop projects for the Department's approval in organised procurement rounds, as opposed to a case-by-case basis (NAO, 2009b). Funding for projects increased.

Local authorities have not been obliged to choose PFI as their procurement route. Where they opted for a PFI project, PFI credits have been available. Prior to 2003, the amount of PFI credits available was limited (NAO, 2009b). Figures reported by the NAO (2009b) show that in 2002 HM Treasury allocated GBP 355 million to Defra for PFI credits, which were then capped at a maximum of GBP 25 million per project. The report notes that the allocation dropped in 2004 to GBP 275 million and the maximum grant allowed increased to GBP 40 million. Following the 2007 Spending Review, the allocation increased substantially to GBP 2 billion and the credits were capped at 50% of a project's capital costs (NAO, 2009b). With better organisation, better support, and better funding, PFI contracts began to increase. As of 2014, the central government had committed GBP 1.7 billion in PFI credits (renamed Waste Infrastructure Credits in 2011) for 28 local authorities' PFI waste infrastructure projects (NAO, 2014; House of Commons, 2014).

PFI waste projects require interaction not only between central and local governments but also between local authorities. Defra has encouraged cross-jurisdictional co-ordination to bring together neighbouring authorities. According to the NAO (2009b:19), "the potential benefits of joint projects are: fewer facilities needing planning permission; economies of scale in project costs; the pooling of risks; and possible operating benefits from a joined up local approach to waste management." Although most projects have involved only a single local authority, there have been some instances of cross-jurisdictional collaboration and (as of 2008) an increasing number of authorities involved in projects under development.

Not all WIDP projects have gone smoothly. Three projects in particular have received a great deal of attention for their failures: those of Surrey, Herefordshire and Worcestershire, and Norfolk County Council. They highlight some issues of multi-level governance in the management of local PFI contracts.

The projects in Herefordshire and Worcestershire (a joint project) and in Surrey were launched in 1998 and 1999 under Defra's predecessor, the Department for Environment, Transport and the Regions (NAO, 2014). At that time the PFI programme was still in its early stages and the approach (in retrospect) proved lax. In this case, the central government agreed to begin grant payments to local authorities when the contractors began to deliver waste management services rather than when they delivered planned assets. Because the local authorities' PFI contracts did not require the contractors to construct all assets before receiving payment, and the Department's contract with the councils did not allow it to unilaterally stop or alter its payments, the Department (and Defra as its successor) ended up paying GBP 213.5 million in PFI credits between 1999 and March 2014, although the main waste assets had not been delivered (House of Commons, 2014). For Herefordshire and Worcestershire, delays resulted from difficulties securing planning permission, uncertainty regarding the final market for waste processing by-product, and problems with financing (resulting from the delays) (NAO, 2014). Problems with financing for Herefordshire and Worcestershire ultimately lead to a transformation of the project such that local authorities opted to act as the sole source of funding for construction (NAO, 2014). In both cases, Defra ultimately changed its payment agreement with local authorities, reducing its funding for both Surrey and for Herefordshire and Worcestershire (NAO, 2014; House of Commons, 2014).

The third problematic waste PFI involves Norfolk County Council. In 2012, Defra agreed to GBP 91 million in PFI credits/grants for a 25-year contract to build an energy-from-waste facility (House of Commons, 2014). It agreed to the funding despite concerns about the council's ability to secure planning permission (House of Commons, 2014). Securing planning permission did ultimately prove highly problematic. The planning application was called in for review by the Secretary of State for Communities and Local Government, and as a result the Council missed the June 2013 deadline for obtaining planning permission set out in its agreement with Defra (NAO, 2014). According to the NAO (2014:18), "when a local authority breaches the terms of its funding agreement, the Department uses [its waste infrastructure capacity model], along with the Programme team's judgement, to decide whether the infrastructure is still needed to meet the EU targets and therefore whether it should continue to offer funding support to the contract". With recognition that the Norfolk facility would not be necessary to meet EU targets, after discussions with the local authority about the likely impact of its decision, Defra revoked the PFI credit funding in October 2013 (NAO, 2014). With planning permission still delayed at the outset of 2014, Norfolk County Council terminated the PFI contract triggering a termination payment of approximately GBP 33.7 million to the contractor (NAO, 2014).

What went wrong? What does it imply about governance arrangements? First, the Surrey and the Herefordshire and Worcestershire projects pre-date the WIDP. Difficulties obtaining planning permission and uncertainty regarding technology are not entirely unexpected for waste infrastructure projects (NAO, 2009b). However, the early contractual arrangements between the local authority and the contractor, and between the local authority and the central government were insufficient. The NAO (2014: 20) found that over time as Defra "gained experience of the issues these projects were likely to encounter, the terms and conditions of its later funding agreements (such as the agreement with Norfolk) became stricter, giving the Department greater scope to reduce or remove funding support". Surrey and Herefordshire and Worcestershire were not the only projects confronting difficulties delivering planned infrastructure. Five "legacy" PFI waste projects were reviewed in 2011 (including Surrey and Herefordshire and Worcestershire) and, in 2013, it was agreed that changes should be pursued to link central government payments with the delivery of the planned infrastructure (NAO, 2014). It is also worth noting that the management of the PFI credits was in regular flux. Over time, responsibility for managing and paying the grants to local authorities was "transferred from the Department for Environment, Transport and the Regions to the Department for Transport, Local Government and the Regions, then to the Office of the Deputy Prime Minister, then to the Department for Communities and Local Government and finally to the Department for Environment, Food & Rural Affairs in April 2011" (NAO, 2014: 9).

With respect to Norfolk, some conclude that Defra demonstrated poor judgement by agreeing to the PFI credits despite early concerns about planning permission, and then later by withdrawing support knowing the risk of termination payments (House of Commons, 2014). Yet blame can be shared with the local authority that failed to attend to Defra's early concerns regarding planning permission and proceeded with a too-optimistic timetable. The impact of the EU targets in this case is interesting. The project was allowed to "fail" after Defra concluded it was not integral to meeting EU targets. This is, in some ways, consistent with Defra's 2010 decision to withdraw provisional grant support (PFI credits) from seven local waste PFI projects in order to save money. Support was withdrawn because the projects were deemed unnecessary to achieve the 2020 EU landfill diversion targets (Defra, 2010). This raises questions about the incentive effects of the EU targets for central government support of possibly problematic local projects that could contribute to landfill targets.

Discussion and conclusions

PFI has played an integral role in delivering a great deal of social infrastructure at the local level in England. As existing literature has documented, at the outset of the PFI programme, local authorities had to confront historical underinvestment in operations and maintenance of capital assets, a poor public track record of delivering infrastructure projects on-time and on-budget, limits to their borrowing for capital expenditures, and the effect of borrowing on the Public Sector Net Debt. The PFI addressed many of these concerns. As of March 2014, there were 728 current PFI projects with a total capital value of GBP 56.6 bn. As noted earlier, much of this new infrastructure may not have occurred without private finance, and analysis suggests that PFI projects tend to outperform traditional procurement in terms of cost and schedule overruns.

PFI's detractors paint a less rosy picture. While the initiative developed much infrastructure, it has also come with costs and challenges. As highlighted at the outset, early PFI deals were delayed by legal issues, problematic bidding procedures, and weak public sector capacity. Reforms were introduced that paved a smoother road for PFI projects going forward. 1999 saw the creation of Partnerships UK to reinforce capacity at all levels of government for PFI deals. PUK, along with PPP units introduced by central government departments, Local Partnerships, and even a local PPP unit (Leeds), facilitated project assessment, standardized contract models, and strengthened local capacity relative to the private sector. Introduction of the Project Review Group, with representation by 4ps, enhanced scrutiny of local projects prior to funding approval. The introduction of and updates to SOPC helped to standardize treatment of risk PFI projects and streamline procurement. The case of WIPD highlights the impact of improved contractual arrangements over time. Yet, despite these efforts criticisms remained: concerns regarding risk allocation, insufficient contract flexibility, a lack of transparency around contingent liabilities, perceived excessive private sector profits; and lengthy procurement timetables led to a reform and rebranding of PFI in 2012. The burden of unitary payments in a tight fiscal environment remains a concern.

What lessons regarding governance emerge from this experience? First, it is worth recalling that public private partnerships represent an alternative to traditional procurement. Well-structured governance arrangements that remove obstacles to successful project design and delivery – from legal impediments to administrative capacity constraints – help make PPPs a viable alternative. However, some multi-level governance arrangements of public private partnerships affect the incentives for PFI uptake and contribute to the success (or weaknesses) of project outcomes. Some mechanisms potentially bias local authorities toward PFI as the preferred approach to procurement. The Eurostat statistical treatment of PPPs creates incentives for all levels of government to structure deals in ways that keep projects from impacting National Accounts. Local government constraints on financing capital expenditures and the PFI credits offered by the central government (which emphasized off-budget treatment of PFI) may well have created an incentive for local governments to emphasize PFI more than they otherwise would have done. Incentive effects of governance arrangements clearly deserve ongoing attention.

Finally, with respect to administrative capacity, many local governments are likely to be at a disadvantage relative to the private sector. Clear efforts have been made to reinforce local authority (and central government) expertise through the introduction of the national PPP unit, line ministry units, 4ps/Local Partnerships, enhanced project scrutiny, and standardisation of contracts. In all likelihood, this has reduced the risk of poorly structured deals and prevented a variety of failures. On the other hand, the experience of indexing in

Scotland, the problematic local waste projects, and the need for deal restructuring among English local authorities reveals the need for continued reinforcement of public sector capacity, including sufficient support once projects are operational.

Notes

1. Navarro-Espigares and Martín-Segura (2011) examine the relationship between PFI investments and regional productivity. They use similar data to this case study (in their case the "PFI signed projects list" published in April 2009 and last consulted by the authors in July 2009) to group the number and value of PFI projects by region and within each region by "promoting authority". In their case promoting authorities are: local authority, health authority, and "other". The authors do not explicitly describe how they assign projects to a "promoting authority". As in this case study, they also examine capital value per capita and unitary charges.
2. Assignment to level of government has been done by the author. This case study differentiates between PPPs undertaken by devolved authorities, NHS, and local authorities in Scotland, Wales, and Northern Ireland. This approach differs from that of HM Treasury, which treats any projects occurring in Scotland, Wales, and Northern Ireland as "devolved".
3. The Lloyd George Avenue and Callaghan Square PFI in Wales was reclassified from "hospitals and acute health" to "roads and highway maintenance."
4. The central government stepped in March 2009 to facilitate project financing and improve market confidence with the introduction of the Infrastructure Finance Unit, which could provide loans to PFI projects on commercial terms (NAO, 2010). Only one loan was made, but an additional 35 projects were able to secure financing suggesting markets did respond favourably to its creation (NAO, 2010).
5. For a detailed discussion of the public governance arrangements for PPPs in the UK, see OECD (2015).
6. There are separate rules for defence and security procurement in the Defence and Security Procurement Directive (2009/81/EC) (LexisPSL and Digings, n.d.)
7. See, for example, the discussion of the sustainable investment rule and PFI in OECD (2009).
8. For the specific incentives created with respect to contract structure, see NAO (2009: 40-41).
9. For an in-depth discussion, see OECD (2015).
10. According to the EPEC (2012a), the first PFIs were facilitated by the Private Finance Panel (PFP), created in 1993 and staffed by (mainly private sector) personnel. The PFP was intended to encourage public and private participation in PFI and troubleshoot problems that might present hurdles to PFI roll-out. It was followed by the "PFI Taskforce" established within HM Treasury following the first government ("Bates") review of PFI progress in 1997. A second review, undertaken in 1999, recommended that the PFI Taskforce be replaced with a permanent support entity, Partnerships UK.

References

4ps (2009), "About us", website, archived at http://webarchive.nationalarchives.gov.uk/20090204152904/ http://4ps.gov.uk/PageContent.aspx?id=28&tp (accessed 24 November 2015).

Audit Scotland (2013), "Major capital investment in councils", March 2013, Edinburgh.

BBC News (2010), "Spending Review: Cuts threaten 12,000 Scottish jobs", 20 Oct 2010, www.bbc.com/news/uk-scotland-11576631 (accessed 4 December 2014).

Booth, L. and V. Starodubtseva (2015), "PFI: costs and benefits", House of Commons, Briefing Paper, No. 6007, 13 May 2015.

Cabinet Office (2015), "Government creates new body to help manage and deliver major projects for UK economy", press release, 11 November 2015, www.gov.uk/government/news/government-creates-new-body-to-help-manage-and-deliver-major-projects-for-uk-economy (accessed 6 December 2015).

Campbell, D. (2012), "NHS trust criticised for 'catalogue of mismanagement' over £411m PFI deal", *The Guardian*, 29 November 2012, www.theguardian.com/society/2012/nov/29/peterborough-nhs-trust-pfi-nao (accessed 25 November 2015).

CEMR (Council of European Municipalities and Regions) (2012), "Local and Regional Government in Europe, Structures and Competences", www.CEMR.org/img/uploads/piecesjointe/filename/local_government_structuresandcompetences_2012_en.pdf (accessed 6 December 2015).

Clark, T., M. Elsby and S. Love (2002), "Trends in British Public Investment", *Fiscal Studies*, Vol. 23, No. 3, pp. 305–342.

Corner, D. (2006), "The United Kingdom Private Finance Initiative: The Challenge of Allocating Risk", *OECD Journal on Budgeting*, Vol. 6, No. 3.

Cuthbert, M. and J. Cuthbert (2011), "The effect of PFI commitments on local authority finances", *Fraser of Allander Economic Commentary*, March 2011, Vol 34 No 3, pp. 53-62.

DCLG (Department for Communities and Local Government) (2010), "Local Authority PFI Projects", Excel, as of February 2010, archived at http://webarchive.nationalarchives.gov.uk/20101012141939/ and www.communities.gov.uk/localgovernment/localgovernmentfinance/pupprivatepartnership/ (accessed 6 October 2015).

Defra (Department for Environment, Food and Rural Affairs) (2010), "Withdrawal of provisional allocation of PFI credits from projects that will now not be needed to meet the 2020 landfill diversion targets", press release, 20 October 2010, www.gov.uk/government/news/changes-to-pfi-programme (accessed 10 December 2015).

Dockreay, A. (2015), "ESA10: EU accounting trouble for Scotland's NPD scheme", IJGlobal, 6 August 2015, https://ijglobal.com/articles/97334/esa10-eu-accounting-trouble-for-scotlands-npd-scheme (accessed 4 December 2015).

EC (European Commission), Economic and Financial Affairs (2015), "Graph of the week: Excessive Deficit Procedure explained", http://ec.europa.eu/economy_finance/graphs/2014-11-10_excessive_deficit_procedure_explained_en.htm (accessed 3 December 2015).

EFA (Education Funding Agency) (2015), "Guidance: Priority School Building Programme: overview", updated 7 August 2015, www.gov.uk/government/publications/psbp-overview/priority-school-building-programme-overview (accessed 17 December 2015).

EPEC (European PPP Expertise Centre) (2015), "Debt and deficit treatment of PPPs according to Eurostat", webpage, The EPEC PPP Guide online, www.eib.org/epec/g2g/i-project-identification/12/125/index.htm (accessed 3 December 2015).

EPEC (2012a), "United Kingdom - England: PPP Units and Related Institutional Framework", European PPP Expertise Centre, www.eib.org/epec/resources/publications/epec_uk_england_public_en.pdf (accessed 12 May 2015).

EPEC (2012b), "United Kingdom - Northern Ireland: PPP Units and Related Institutional Framework", European PPP Expertise Centre, www.eib.org/epec/resources/publications/epec_uk_scotland_public_en.pdf (accessed 12 May 2015).

EPEC (2012c), "United Kingdom - Scotland: PPP Units and Related Institutional Framework", European PPP Expertise Centre, www.eib.org/epec/resources/publications/epec_uk_scotland_public_en.pdf (accessed 12 May 2015).

EPEC (2010), "Eurostat Treatment of Public-Private Partnerships: Purposes, Methodology and Recent Trends", European PPP Expertise Centre, www.eib.org/epec/resources/epec-eurostat-statistical-treatment-of-ppps.pdf (accessed 3 December 2015).

HM Treasury (2014a), "Current projects as at 31 March 2014", Excel, www.gov.uk/government/uploads/system/uploads/attachment_data/file/387225/current_projects_as_at_31_March_2014.xlsx (accessed 14 July 2015).

HM Treasury (2014b), "Private Finance Initiative projects: 2014 summary data", December 2014, London.

HM Treasury (2014c), "National Infrastructure Plan 2014", December 2014.

HM Treasury (2012), "A new approach to public private partnerships", London, UK.

HM Treasury (2007), "Standardisation of PFI Contracts, Version 4", March 2007, http://webarchive.nationalarchives.gov.uk/20130410173120/ and http://hm-treasury.gov.uk/d/pfi_sopc4pu101_210307.pdf (accessed 8 December 2015).

House of Commons, Committee of Public Accounts (2014), "The Department for Environment, Food and Rural Affairs: oversight of three PFI waste projects", September 2014.

House of Commons, Treasury Committee (2011), "Private Finance Initiative", Seventeenth Report of Session 2010–12, HC 1146, August 2011.

House of Lords (2010), "Private Finance Projects and off-balance sheet debt, Volume I: Report", House of Lords Select Committee on Economic Affairs, 17 March 2010.

Istrate, E. and R. Puentes (2011), "Moving Forward on Public Private Partnerships: U.S. and International Experience with PPP Units", Brookings-Rockefeller Project on State and Metropolitan Innovation, December 2011, www.brookings.edu/~/media/research/files/papers/2011/12/08 transportation istrate puentes/1208_transportation_istrate_puentes.pdf and www.brookings.edu/wp-content/uploads/2016/06/1208_transportation_istrate_puentes.pdf (accessed 3 April 2017).

LexisPSL (n.d.), "The National Infrastructure Plan", LexisPSL Practice Note, www.lexisnexis.com/uk/lexispsl/bankingandfinance/document/391375/5CNW-YG61-F186-J05N-00000-00s (accessed 4 June 2015).

LexisPSL and Addleshaw Goddard (n.d.-a), "Introduction to the Private Finance Initiative and Public Private Partnerships", LexisPSL Practice Note, www.lexisnexis.com/uk/lexispsl/bankingandfinance/document/391290/5D5H-YVP1-F185-S3W8-00000-00 (accessed 4 June 2015).

LexisPSL and Addleshaw Goddard (n.d.-b), "PFI--UK developments and reform", LexisPSL Practice Note, www.lexisnexis.com/uk/lexispsl/bankingandfinance/document/391290/5D5H-YVP1-F185-S4N3-00000-00 (accessed 4 June 2015).

LexisPSL and Addleshaw Goddard (n.d.-c), "UK infrastructure projects--relevant sources, government bodies and guidance", LexisPSL Practice Note. www.lexisnexis.com/uk/lexispsl/bankingand finance/document/391290/5D5H-YVP1-F185-S4CK-00000-00 (accessed 4 June 2015).

LexisPSL and Addleshaw Goddard (n.d.-d), "Forms of Public Private Partnerships", LexisPSL Practice Note; www.lexisnexis.com/uk/lexispsl/bankingandfinance/document/391290/5D5H-YVP1-F185-S4MR-00000-00/Forms%20of%20Public%20Private%20Partnerships (accessed 4 June 2015).

LexisPSL and Digings, L. (n.d.), "Procurement law", LexisPSL Practice Note, www.lexisnexis.com/uk/lexispsl/bankingandfinance/document/393985/55MK-3T41-F18D-K15G-00000-00/ (accessed 4 June 2015).

LexisPSL and Laver, N. (2013), "PF2--the story so far", LexisPSL News Analysis. www.lexisnexis.com/uk/lexispsl/bankingandfinance/document/391370/595Y-7FM1-F186-50M6-00000-00 (accessed 4 June 2015).

LexisPSL and Laver, N. (2012), "PF2--a new look for PFI?", LexisPSL News Analysis, www.lexisnexis.com/uk/lexispsl/bankingandfinance/document/391288/576R-38H1-F186-P3NF-00000-00 (accessed 4 June 2015).

Local Partnerships (2016), "Efficiency – A commercial approach to achieve savings", http://localpartnerships.org.uk/wp-content/uploads/2016/08/Efficiency-A-commercial-approach-to-achieve-savings.pdf (accessed 6 Feb 2017).

Local Partnerships (n.d.), "Case Study: Contract review - energy management, Newcastle & North Tyneside Street Lighting", London, http://localpartnerships.org.uk/images/files/Case_Study_-_Newcastle__North_Tyneside_-_Energy_Management.pdf (accessed 24 Oct 2015)

NAO (National Audit Office) (2015a), "A Short Guide to the NAO's work on local authorities", July 2015.

NAO (2015b), "A Short Guide to the Department for Communities and Local Government", July 2015.

NAO (2014), "Department for Environment, Food & Rural Affairs, Oversight of three PFI waste projects", report by the Comptroller and Auditor General, HC 264 Session 2014-2015, 17 June 2014.

NAO (2011), "Lessons from PFI and other projects", report by the Comptroller and Auditor General, HC 920 Session 2010-2012, 15 April 2011.

NAO (2010), "Financing PFI projects in the credit crisis and the Treasury's response", report by the Comptroller and Auditor General, HC 287 Session 2010-2011, 27 July 2010.

NAO (2009a), "Private Finance Projects", a paper prepared for the Lords Economic Affairs Committee, October 2009.

NAO (2009b), "Department for Environment, Food & Rural Affairs, Managing the waste PFI programme", report by the Comptroller and Auditor General, 14 January 2009.

National Records of Scotland (2014), "Population Projections for Scottish Areas (2012-based)", Excel, www.nrscotland.gov.uk/statistics-and-data/statistics/statistics-by-theme/population/population-projections/sub-national-population-projections/2012-based/list-of-tables (accessed 12 October 2015).

Navarro-Espigares, J.L. and J.A. Martín-Segura (2011), "Public–private partnership and regional productivity in the UK", *The Service Industries Journal*, 31:4, 559-580, http://dx.doi.org/10.1080/02642069.2010.504303.

Northern Ireland Executive (2015), "Local government reform", webpage, www.nidirect.gov.uk/index/information-and-services/government-citizens-and-rights/government/local-government/local-government-reform.htm (accessed 6 December 2015).

OECD (2015), "OECD Review of Public Governance of Public-Private Partnerships in the United Kingdom", OECD, April 2015, https://www.oecd.org/governance/procurement/toolbox/search/oecd-review-public-governance-ppp-uk.pdf.

OECD (2009), *OECD Economic Surveys: United Kingdom 2009*, OECD Publishing, Paris, http://dx.doi.org/10.1787/eco_surveys-gbr-2009-en

OECD, UK regional population statistics (TL2) 1992-2012, Excel, extracted from OECD.stat 12 October 2015.

ONS (Office of National Statistics) (2015), "MYE2: Population Estimates by single year of age and sex for local authorities in the UK, mid-2014", Excel, version 25 June 2015.

ONS (2014), "Table 1: 2012-based Subnational Population Projections for Regions in England", last updated 29 May 2014, Excel, www.ons.gov.uk/ons/rel/snpp/sub-national-population-projections/2012-based-projections/index.html (accessed 12 October 2015).

ONS (2006), "Government and public sector debt measures", September 2006, www.ons.gov.uk/ons/guide-method/method-quality/specific/economy/public-sector-finances/government-and-public-sector-debt-measures.pdf (accessed 10 December 2015).

Partnerships Bulletin (2007), "Page Turner", 30 August 2007, www.partnershipsbulletin.com/interviews/view/4 (accessed 24 November 2015).

Pisu, M., B. Pels and N. Bottini (2015), "Improving infrastructure in the United Kingdom", *OECD Economics Department Working Papers*, No. 1244, OECD Publishing, Paris, http://dx.doi.org/10.1787/5jrxqbqc7m0p-en.

PriceWaterhouseCoopers (PWC) (2011), "Is PFI working? Buying excellent, settling for average", Talking Points, http://hb.betterregulation.com/external/Is%20PFI%20working%20Buying%20excellent,%20settling%20for%20average.pdf (accessed 9 December 2015).

PUK (Partnerships UK) (2009), "What we do", webpage, archived at http://webarchive.nationalarchives.gov.uk/20110518155402/ and www.partnershipsuk.org.uk/What-PUK-Do.aspx (accessed 10 December 2015).

Scottish Government (2015), "About Local Government in Scotland", www.gov.scot/Topics/Government/local-government/localg (accessed 6 December 2015).

SFT (Scottish Futures Trust) (2015a), "SFTinvest", www.scottishfuturestrust.org.uk/our-work/funding-and-finance (accessed 7 December 2015).

SFT (2015b), "Non-Profit Distributing (NPD)", www.scottishfuturestrust.org.uk/our-work/funding-and-finance/non-profit-distributing/ (accessed 3 December 2015).

SocInvest (2012), "Reforming PFI: Lessons from Scotland", 10 October 2012, www.socinvest.co.uk/news/3465/Reforming-PFI-Lessons-from-Scotland (accessed 3 December 2015).

StatsWales (2013), "2012-based national population projections for Wales, 2012-2037", Excel, last updated November 2013, https://statswales.wales.gov.uk/Catalogue/Population-and-Migration/Population/Projections/National/2012-Based/PopulationProjections-by-Year-Gender (accessed 12 October 2015).

UK Office of Budget Responsibility (2015), PSF Aggregates Databank, Excel, November 2015, http://budgetresponsibility.org.uk/data/ (accessed 9 December 2015).

Vernon, P. and J. Sanders (2007), "The Move Towards Batched Projects", in the *International Comparative Legal Guide to PFI / PPP Projects 2007*, Global Legal Group Ltd., London, pp. 1-6.

Welsh Government (2015a), "Unitary authorities", http://gov.wales/topics/localgovernment/unitary-authorities/?lang=en (accessed 6 December 2015).

Welsh Government (2015b), "Wales Infrastructure Investment Plan", webpage, updated 23 June 2015, http://gov.wales/funding/wiipindex/?lang=en (accessed 14 December 2015).

Wilson, D. and C. Game (2011), *Local Government in the United Kingdom*, 5th Edition, Palgrave MacMillan.

Winch, G. M. (2012), "30 Years of private finance in the United Kingdom", in Winch, G.M., Onishi, M. and S. Schmidt (eds.) (2012), *Taking Stock of PPP and PFI Around the World*, Vol. Report No. 126, London: Association of Chartered Certified Accountants, pp. 117-125.

Winch, G.M., M. Onishi and S. Schmidt (eds.) (2012), *Taking Stock of PPP and PFI Around the World*, Vol. Report No. 126, London: Association of Chartered Certified Accountants.

Chapter 4. Public-private partnerships for infrastructure at the subnational level of government: Opportunities and challenges in the Commonwealth of Virginia, United States

by Jonathan Gifford and Morghan Transue

This chapter presents a case study of public-private partnerships (PPPs) for infrastructure development in the state of Virginia, United States. As one of the first US states to enable PPP procurement, Virginia's more than 25-year history with PPPs and their governance provide a unique opportunity to study subnational governments' challenges and success factors in practice. The case study focuses in particular on five categories of challenges: (i) Intergovernmental regulatory coherence; (ii) Financial risks; (iii) Cross-jurisdictional co-ordination; (iv)Administrative capacity and (v) Accountability and transparency. The case study concludes with a summary of Virginia's major PPP drivers, challenges, and success factors, along with a discussion of lessons learned that can inform other subnational governments.

Introduction

As governments throughout the world strive to develop, operate, and maintain infrastructure assets to support their citizens' well-being, procurement practices have advanced beyond traditional approaches. As a result, many governments have turned to alternative procurement approaches to fill resource gaps. Recognising this trend, Principle 6 of the OECD's 2014 Council Recommendation on Effective Public Investment Across Levels of Government notes the potential benefits when government actors, including those at the subnational level, match private financing and expertise with public investment needs and administrative capacity through arrangements including public-private partnerships (PPPs) (OECD, 2014). While such PPP approaches present great potential value, they differ significantly from traditional approaches and often introduce highly complex features and a different allocation of risks. As a result, PPPs offer important opportunities but also important challenges for subnational governments engaged in infrastructure development and delivery.

To develop a greater understanding of the opportunities, challenges, and key support characteristics involved in successful subnational PPP governance, the following discussion explores an example of the United States' PPP experience through a case study in the Commonwealth of Virginia. As one of the first US states to enable PPP procurement, Virginia's more than 25-year history with PPPs and their governance provide a unique opportunity to study subnational governments' challenges and success factors in practice (Buxbaum and Ortiz, 2009: 9).

The case study proceeds as follows. The next section explores the current state of play in the US, focusing on infrastructure needs, the role of subnational governments in addressing these needs, and recent trends in PPP procurement. This is followed by examination of the Virginia PPP experience, with attention to five categories of challenges:

1. Intergovernmental regulatory coherence;
2. Financial risks;
3. Cross-jurisdictional co-ordination;
4. Administrative capacity; and
5. Accountability and transparency.

The case study concludes with a summary of Virginia's major PPP drivers, challenges, and success factors, along with a discussion of lessons learned that can inform other subnational governments.[1]

The US context: Infrastructure needs, PPPs, and the role of subnational governments

With its large, diverse, and post-industrialised economy, its nearly 320 million residents (US Census Bureau, 2015a), and its large and varied geographic area, the United States faces many challenges in developing and maintaining its extensive infrastructure systems. Evaluating the US legacy systems and future needs across fifteen infrastructure categories, the American Society of Civil Engineers' "2017 Infrastructure Report Card" estimated that USD 4.6 trillion in new investment would be needed by 2025 to address the country's infrastructure capacity, operation and maintenance, safety, and resilience needs (American Society of Civil Engineers, 2017: 8). With nearly 100 000 miles of rail and more than 4 million miles of roadways, 10 000 miles of transit, 5 000 public-use airports, 185 000 miles of oil pipeline, and 1.5 million miles of gas pipeline, public infrastructure investment represents a significant undertaking for US subnational governments (USDOT 2015a; 2015b).

The US federal system of government operates under a decentralised structure with authority divided between the federal government, fifty state governments, and thousands of city, county, and other municipal and local governments. Infrastructure provision responsibilities are particularly fragmented, with primary authority resting with subnational governments. As in many other OECD countries, subnational governments in the US account for the bulk of total public investment (55.2% in 2014) (OECD, 2016). Looking at transportation and water infrastructure, US states and local governments accounted for 62% of capital spending in 2014 (US Congressional Budget Office, 2015). For example, since the early 19th century, subnational governments have maintained primary responsibility for roadway provision, although some federal funding programmes developed during the early 20th century. The federal government's funding role in highway provision increased substantially during the mid-20th century when the National Interstate and Defense Highway Act (1956) and the Federal Highway Trust Fund provided 90% or more in federal funding for interstate highway construction. Maintenance funding responsibility remained with the states, however (Seely, 1987; Gifford, 2003). While the interstate highway system represents an exceptional case of federal financial support, federal regulatory frameworks do address environmental protection, community impacts, hazardous material, and vehicle safety concerns. State and local governments maintain primary authority for assessing and addressing their citizens' infrastructure needs. This arrangement limits centralised planning and control, but provides enhanced opportunities for locally appropriate solutions, experimentation, and citizen engagement.

In the US infrastructure sector, the term public-private partnership encompasses a range of contract types that shift facility construction, funding, financing, operation, and/or maintenance activities to private partners (Custos and Reitz, 2010: 555; FHWA, n.d. c). Starting in the late 1980s, US PPPs began to increase private-sector participation compared to traditional design-bid-build (DBB) approaches, bundling design, construction, financing, operation, and/or maintenance phases into single private-sector delivery agreements. While the public sector usually retains facility ownership, PPP arrangements typically rely on private partners to make significant investments, allowing them to raise revenue through tolls, user fees, and/or public payments (US General Accounting Office, 1999: 13–14). Such PPP structures include, but are not limited to: design-build (DB); private service and/or maintenance contracts; design-build-operate-maintain (DBOM); build-operate-transfer (BOT); build-transfer-operate (BTO); design-build-finance (DBF); design-build-finance-operate (DBFO); design-build-finance-operate-maintain (DBFOM); and long-term lease agreements or concessions (brownfield) (FHWA, n.d.c; Buxbaum and Ortiz, 2009: 8). These public-private arrangements offer access to private capital, financing, and expertise, along with a range of time saving, cost saving, and quality improving benefits derived from: a) private-sector incentives for on-time delivery, facility quality, and life-cycle efficiencies; b) cost, scheduling, and revenue risk-transfers; and c) innovative technologies and techniques (Rall, Reed, and Farber, 2010: 9–10).

Between 2007 and 2013, transportation PPP projects accounted for about USD 22.7 billion in public and private funds, or about 2% of total capital highway investments in the United States over that period (USDOT, 2015c: 173). Specifically, funding for transportation PPP projects in the US market comes from two primary sources: user fee revenues (tolls, fares) and government appropriations. In addition, financing arrangements generally fall into two categories: revenue risk and availability payment (AP). For revenue risk projects, a significant portion of the financing depends on toll revenues for repayment, which, in turn, depend on future traffic. For AP projects, in contrast, the government promises to pay the concessionaire a fee subject to the concessionaire's delivery (i.e. making available) of a properly operated and maintained facility. The concessionaire takes "appropriation risk," that is, the risk that the government will fail to appropriate the funds to make its payment. On the other hand, the concessionaire also retains the ability to curtail access (i.e. availability) of the facility if the government fails to pay. States vary in how they register these availability payment obligations on their balance sheets. Some states consider all such obligations as debt and record liabilities. Others allow the exclusion of such future contractual obligations from balance sheets. Rating agency treatment of availability payments is tending toward including them as a factor in assessing issuer creditworthiness (Hecht, 2015).

Recognising the potential offered by innovative delivery approaches, the US federal government began supporting state-level PPP experimentation nationwide in the 1990s. Highway provision provides an illustrative example. As road networks expanded during the mid-20th century, states turned from in-house design approaches to DBB processes in which public agencies procured project designs from private engineering firms and bid out project construction. By the early 1990s, however, growing dissatisfaction over cost and schedule over-runs, poor facility quality, and deferred maintenance drove advancements in state of the art project delivery strategies. The federal government undertook several actions to support these innovative procurement approaches. For example, the Federal Highway Administration (FHWA) established Special Experimental Project Number 14 (SEP-14) in 1990, allowing states to experiment with innovative procurement methods for projects supported by federal funds. By 2002, 140 highway capital projects worth USD 5.5 billion[2] resulted from DB approaches supported by this programme (US General Accounting Office, 1997; FHWA, 2006).

More recently, the US Department of Transportation (USDOT) established several federal programmes supporting innovative procurement strategies, private-sector involvement, and PPPs at the subnational level. For example, the FHWA formed its Innovative Program Delivery office in 2008 to offer tools, resources, technical assistance, outreach, and other support for communities considering innovative procurement, delivery, and financing approaches (FHWA, n.d. b). In addition, the department formed the Build America Transportation Investment Center (BATIC) in 2015 to support communities pursuing P3 approaches for transportation infrastructure projects across all modes (USDOT, 2015d). National-level professional organisations also provide P3-related resources and support, including the National Conference of State Legislatures' Public-Private Partnerships for Transportation: A Toolkit for Legislators (Rall, Reed, and Farber, 2010; Rall, 2014) and the American Association of State Highway and Transportation Officials' Transportation Finance Clearinghouse (American Association of State Highway and Transportation Officials, 2015). The US Economic Development Administration provides non-infrastructure grants to subnational partners for capacity building on PPP and general infrastructure delivery. Similarly, the National Governors Association has also offered workshops and resources for state officials (National Governors Association Center for Best Practices, n.d.).

While the US federal government supports procurement experimentation and alternative financing at the subnational level, the United States lacks a national PPP statutory framework. Instead, states maintain primary responsibility for allowing PPP approaches and establishing PPP programmes (Rall, Reed, and Farber, 2010: 15). As of July 2015, thirty-three states, the District of Columbia, and Puerto Rico enacted statutes enabling

PPP approaches for transportation infrastructure delivery (FHWA, n.d.d). PPPs for "social infrastructure" (e.g. hospitals, schools, and public facilities) remain much less common in the United States. Unlike water, wastewater, or transportation projects, such facilities rarely qualify for favourable treatment under the federal funding programmes and tax policies discussed in more detail below (US House of Representatives, 2014: 18, 34).

State statutory frameworks and PPP programmes vary considerably, ranging in programme scope, policy and geographic objectives, allowable proposals (e.g. solicited vs. unsolicited), qualifying facilities, qualifying partners, allowable delivery mechanisms, and implementing agencies (Buxbaum and Ortiz, 2009: 13–15, 27; Rall, Reed, and Farber, 2010: 11, 13, 41–59). A diverse PPP project history has arisen from this statutory diversity. Between 1989 and 2011, the United States developed 96 transportation PPP projects collectively valued at USD 54.3 billion. Three quarters of this investment occurred in eight states: Texas (USD 9.57 billion); California (USD 6.02 billion); Florida (USD 4.63 billion); Colorado (USD 4.85 billion); Indiana (USD 3.85 billion); Virginia (USD 3.88 billion); Utah (USD 3.66 billion); and New Jersey (USD 3.35 billion) (Reinhardt, 2011: 25-26). These eight states represent large economies, long PPP programme histories, and/or favourable statutory frameworks for PPPs. Favourable statutory frameworks, in turn, develop in states with higher traffic congestion due to state legislators' focus on the problem (Geddes and Wagner, 2013). During the 1989 to 2011 period, states have generally preferred DB, DBF, or DBOM approaches, building 79 projects worth USD 31.5 billion using these arrangements, although 11 projects worth USD 12.4 billion employed DBFOM or concession contracts. The remaining four projects, worth USD 6.9 billion, involved asset privatisations (Reinhardt, 2011: 25–26).

PPPs will likely remain an increasingly popular alternative to traditional design-bid-build procurement as infrastructure needs develop, existing facilities age, maintenance costs rise, and capital expenditures fall. Between 2003 and 2014, for example, US inflation-adjusted public spending on transportation and water infrastructure fell by 23% for capital projects but increased 6% for operation and maintenance (US Congressional Budget Office, 2015: 12).

The US federal government offers a variety of grant and loan programmes for subnational infrastructure investment, many of which are supported by the Highway Trust Fund. Originally established in 1956 to fund the interstate highway system, this fund today uses federal fuel tax revenue to fund 25% of all national transit and highway investment. Unfortunately, inflation and improving vehicle fuel efficiencies have eroded the fuel tax base, forcing the fund to the brink of insolvency in recent years. Without sufficient political will to raise federal fuel taxes, the government has preserved the fund's solvency through a chain of multi-billion dollar stopgap measures drawing from the general fund (FHWA, 2014d; Morris, 2015; Halsey and Eilperin, 2014; Rubin, 2015). The most recent surface transportation authorisation, the FAST Act (Fixing America's Surface Transportation Act, Pub. Law 114-94), signed into law on December 4, 2015, maintains this policy. The act did not raise fuel taxes and authorised supports the Highway Trust Fund with approximately USD 70 billion in transfers from the general fund.

Many states have similar revolving funds and state infrastructure banks facing parallel challenges (Puentes and Thompson, 2012; Gifford, 2010). With their strong reliance on federal funds and tax revenues (see Figure 4.1. for the highway sector), state and local infrastructure programmes have also struggled to find sufficient funds to address their infrastructure needs through traditional sources.

Figure 4.1.State highway funding

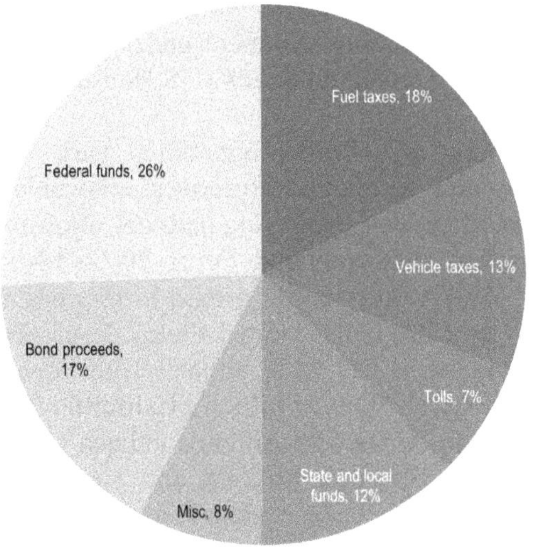

Sources: US Federal Highway Administration (FHWA 2014c), "Highway Statistics 2013: Revenues Used by Local Government for Highways – 2012", www.fhwa.dot.gov/policyinformation/statistics/2013/lgf1.cfm; FHWA (2014e). "Highway Statistics 2013: Revenues Used By States for Highways – 2013", www.fhwa.dot.gov/policyinformation/statistics/2013/sf1.cfm#foot1.

Figure 4.2. Local highway funding

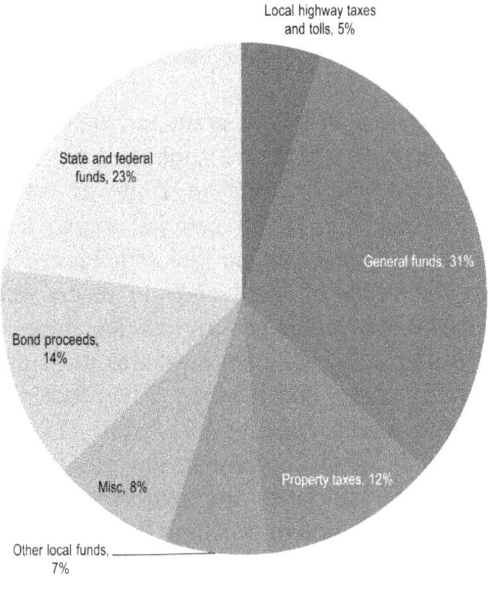

Sources: US Federal Highway Administration (FHWA 2014c), "Highway Statistics 2013: Revenues Used by Local Government for Highways – 2012",www.fhwa.dot.gov/policyinformation/statistics/2013/lgf1.cfm; FHWA (2014e). "Highway Statistics 2013: Revenues Used By States for Highways – 2013", www.fhwa.dot.gov/policyinformation/statistics/2013/sf1.cfm#foot1.

Beyond its traditional grant and loan programmes, the federal government also offers several programmes and policies that support innovative financing. The Transportation Infrastructure Finance and Innovation Act of 1998 (TIFIA), for example, provides credit assistance for large transportation projects. This programme became particularly attractive following the 2008 financial crisis. In addition, 2005's Safe, Accountable, Flexible, Efficient Transportation Equity Act: A Legacy for Users (SAFETEA-LU) included provisions allowing tax-exempt Private Activity Bonds (PAB) for up to USD 15 billion in selected highway and freight projects developed and operated by private parties (FHWA, 2015). Similarly, the American Reinvestment and Recovery Act of 2009 created Build America Bonds (BAB) following the 2008 financial crisis to provide subsidised municipal financing. The programme expired in December 2010, but enabled 2 275 BAB issues supporting more than USD 181 billion in public infrastructure projects (US Treasury Department, 2011).

Finally, federal and state municipal bond policies exempt interest paid on bonds issued by subnational governments (including Puerto Rico) from federal and state income taxes. This represents a distinct feature of the US infrastructure financing system and as a result, interest rates for municipal debt have typically been lower than for taxable debt. In addition, the US municipal bond market is large — USD 3.7 trillion in mid-2015 — and liquid, serving as a principal source of capital for states and localities (US House of Representatives, 2014: 10). However, states typically cap their bond issuance in order to protect their bond ratings. As a result, competition within a state for access to state and municipal bond funds is often fierce, limiting the debt capacity available for transportation infrastructure investment. In addition, interest paid by PPPs is often taxable under federal or local law, leading to higher market rates for PPP project debt (for a more detailed discussion of project finance see, for example, Esty 2003). Note, however, that the Internal Revenue Service's (IRS) Rule 63-20 and Revenue Proclamation 82-26 have allowed non-profit public-benefit corporations to issue tax-exempt municipal bonds, opening another financing option for PPPs (US Securities and Exchange Commission, 2012; FHWA, n.d.a).

Subnational PPPs: The Virginia case

The Commonwealth of Virginia, located on the US mid-Atlantic coast, was first settled at Jamestown in 1607, making it one of the 13 original American colonies ("Virginia - US States", 2015). Its legislative body, the Virginia General Assembly, established as the House of Burgesses in 1619, represents the oldest continuous law-making body with elected representatives in the new world (Virginia General Assembly, n.d.). The state also boasts the first American highway legislation (1632) and arguably the first American toll road (1772) (VDOT, 2006: 5, 10). Today, the state covers 39 490 square miles (102 280 sq. km), with a population of over 8 million people (US Census Bureau, 2015b) and a primarily service-based economy (Table 4.1).

Table 4.1. Virginia GDP by industry group (2014)

Industry	GDP (USD millions)	% of total state GDP
Finance, Insurance, Real Estate, Rental, and Leasing	90 765	20%
Government	86 462	19%
Professional and Business Services	84 891	18%
Construction and Manufacturing	59 349	13%
Other Services	43 932	9%
Wholesale and Retail Trade	43 620	9%
Education, Health Care, and Social Assistance	32 154	7%
Utilities and Transportation	17 964	4%
Mining and Natural Resources	4 476	1%
Total	463 613	100%

Source: US Bureau of Economic Analysis (2014), "Regional Data, GDP & Personal Income", www.bea.gov/iTable/index_regional.cfm.

PPP drivers and statutory history

Virginia's recent history with alternative infrastructure procurement originated in 1986 when Governor Gerald L. Baliles identified transportation infrastructure development as a top priority for his administration (Virginia General Assembly, 1986: 15–25). A specially-formed Commission on Transportation in the 21st Century (COT-21) evaluated the state's transportation needs and funding options and ultimately identified USD 7 billion in needed transportation investment (USD 15 billion in 2015 dollars). At the same time, private actors submitted draft legislation permitting privately-funded toll road development in the state. Following the Commission's recommendation to the state legislature, this draft developed into Virginia's first PPP enabling statute, the Virginia Highway Corporation Act of 1988 (HCA) (Levy, 1996).

Enacted with the intent of accelerating roadway construction and improving cost efficiencies, HCA permitted the submission of proposals by private parties for toll-based roadway construction and operation. The state's Commonwealth Transportation Board reviewed and approved the proposals' locations, designs, costs, interconnection requirements, and public needs assessments, while the Virginia Department of Transportation (VDOT) arranged comprehensive agreements for facility inspections. The State Corporation Commission (SCC) then reviewed the proposals; if approved, the private partners received certificates of authority allowing them to construct and operate their toll road facility for up to ten years following the original permanent financing's term. To protect the public interest, the SCC regulated the resulting facilities and authorised tolls. Upon termination, facility ownership reverted to the state.

Five years after HCA, in 1993, the state legislature, the Virginia General Assembly, began re-evaluating the state's procurement processes, establishing the Joint Subcommittee Studying Privatisation of Certain State Government Functions to consider infrastructure project and highway maintenance privatisation among other government activities (Virginia General Assembly, 1993; 1994). As the Joint Subcommittee developed its findings, the General Assembly passed the Qualifying Transportation Facilities Act of 1994 (QTFA), allowing PPP procurement for a wider range of qualifying transportation facilities and shifting primary proposal review from the SCC to whatever "responsible public entity" had "the power to acquire, construct or improve the applicable transportation facility." Nevertheless, approved projects still required SCC certification and remained under its regulatory authority as public service commissions or utilities.

The Joint Subcommittee's final report, issued in May 1995, proposed several changes to the new QTFA statutory framework. It first recommended that responsible public entities assume sole responsibility for project approvals, limiting SCC involvement to regulating comprehensive agreement terminations under default conditions. The report then recommended allowing public entities to solicit PPPs through requests for proposals (RFP). It also recommended clearly exempting qualifying PPP facilities from the state's public procurement laws (Virginia General Assembly, Joint Subcommittee Studying Privatisation of Certain State Government Functions, 1995: 3–5). In response, the General Assembly quickly amended and re-titled QTFA to create the Public-Private Transportation Act of 1995 (PPTA).

PPTA addressed most of the Joint Subcommittee recommendations, adjusting the qualifying facility definition, permitting public-agency PPP RFPs, shifting proposal approvals and oversight from the SCC to responsible public entities (including user-fee setting and termination dates), exempting PPPs from the Virginia Public Procurement Act, and removing the ten-year concession limitation. Looking to extend the state's PPP programme to a broader range of infrastructure sectors, seven years later the Virginia General Assembly passed the Public-Private Education Facilities and Infrastructure Act of 2002 (PPEA), replicating PPTA's PPP procurement statutes for educational, governmental, and other public infrastructure facilities.

The steady expansion of Virginia's PPP statutes reflects the changing environment influencing its infrastructure sector over the past several decades. Growing urban population centres, for instance, have increased traffic congestion and project complexity as new projects are developed to respond to high population densities and existing facilities. The highway capacity expansions developed under the 495 Express Lanes project, for example, had to accommodate the quarter million vehicles already travelling in the existing lanes (Samuel, 2013). Newly relevant alternative transportation modes (e.g. bikes, buses) and land use policies (e.g. transit-oriented development) have also contributed to increased project complexity and inter-governmental co-ordination requirements. Increasing costs, rising consumer expectations, and technological innovations have also complicated Virginia's infrastructure investment environment and disrupted traditional procurement processes (Gifford et al., 2015b).

Such challenges will likely persist into Virginia's future. Policy makers anticipate a growing but aging population, especially in urban northern Virginia, Fredericksburg, Richmond, and Hampton Roads. They also foresee a shift from automobile reliance to a more multi-modal and rail-based transportation system, along with continued need for technological, user information, sustainability, and resilience enhancements. To address these needs, their infrastructure investment plans stress return-on-investment optimisation; safety, security, and resiliency improvements; more efficient programme delivery; operational improvements and demand management; improved transparency and accountability; and improved land use and facility co-ordination (Virginia Office of Intermodal Planning and Investment, 2015: 19–21, 26–28, 33).

Despite these challenges and investment needs, public infrastructure budgets and bond issues have not grown commensurately. The 2008 economic downturn particularly diminished revenues from sales taxes, and motor vehicle sales and use taxes, which account for about a third of Virginia's transportation funding. While the American Recovery and Reinvestment Act of 2009 provided nearly USD 700 million in highway stimulus funding (VDOT, 2012a), state and federal programmes using motor fuel taxes to support about half of the state's transportation funding have become less reliable as inflation and increased fuel efficiencies erode the tax base (Virginia Office of Intermodal Planning and Investment, 2010: 64–66). Considering the state's increasingly complex infrastructure needs and stagnating funds, the private-sector development, funding, financing, and management options offered by PPP procurement arrangements present appealing solutions.

PPP project experience

Given Virginia's long history with transportation-related PPP statutes under HCA, QTFA, and PPTA, transportation infrastructure projects offer some of its largest and most visible PPP endeavours, although the programme is currently considering a range of PPP development opportunities related to air rights, solar energy, broadband, cell towers, advertising, interstate lighting upgrades, customer service facilities, and airport runway maintenance (VAP3, 2015f). While PPEA has supported a range of public and educational facilities at the local level, these smaller, typically design-build projects have not been documented systematically given the many state and local entities arranging the partnerships. As a result, the following case analysis draws primarily from transportation projects (see Table 4.2) to explore five categories of challenges facing subnational governments engaged in PPP infrastructure development: 1) intergovernmental regulatory coherence; 2) financial risks; 3) cross-jurisdictional co-ordination; 4) administrative capacity; and 5) accountability and transparency.

Intergovernmental regulatory coherence

PPP statutory frameworks and regulations that vary across federal and subnational governments can complicate investment environments for potential private partners, raising business costs and discouraging their participation (Mizell and Allain-Dupré, 2013: 37). In the US, complex interactions between large infrastructure projects and state and federal environmental protection statutes present the most compelling example (Custos and Reitz, 2010: 571), often delaying projects and greatly increasing total project costs (e.g. see Virginia's 495 Express Lanes Case, Daito et al., 2013; or California's South Bay Expressway case, Gifford, Bolaños, and Daito, 2014). In addition, the state-based US PPP market, despite guidance and support from federal programmes, offers a highly variable and confusing operating environment for private actors navigating the range of proposal, financing, facility, partner, and institutional regulations maintained by each state (Istrate and Puentes, 2011: 8; Rall, Reed, and Farber, 2010: 41–59).

Table 4.2. Virginia transportation PPP project history

Completed	Under construction
Dulles Greenway	Elizabeth River Crossings
I-495 Capital Beltway Express Lanes	Route 58 Tri-County & Laurel Forks
Route 895, Pocahontas Parkway	Coalfields Expressway
Route 199	Route 28
Route 58	Dulles Rail
Route 288	
I-95 Express Lanes	
	Under procurement
	I-66 Transformation
	Route 460
	Odd Fellows Road Interchange
	I-73 Corridor
	NOVA Commuter Fast Ferry Service
	NOCA North-South Connector
	I-95 Statewide Corridor Improvements
	I-64 Corridor Improvements
	Port of Virginia
	Southeastern Parkway & Greenbelt
	Powhite Parkway Extension
	Western Washington Bypass
Under consideration	No longer under consideration
I-495 Express Lanes Extension	Route 460
I-66 Corridor Park-and-Ride System Enhancements	Odd Fellows Road Interchange
Statewide Rest Area & Parking Asset Enhancements	I-73 Corridor
Hampton Roads Crossings Improvements	NOVA Commuter Fast Ferry Service
Route 460/58 Connector	NOCA North-South Connector
Patriots Crossing	I-95 Statewide Corridor Improvements
I-64 to HOT	I-64 Corridor Improvements
	Port of Virginia
	Southeastern Parkway & Greenbelt
	Powhite Parkway Extension
	Western Washington Bypass

Source: Virginia Office of Public-Private Partnerships (VAP3) (2013), "Public-Private Transportation Act Projects", www.p3virginia.org/wp-content/uploads/2014/12/2013_PPTA_Portfolio_Map_final1.pdf; VAP3 (2015), "Projects", webpage, www.p3virginia.org/p3-projects; VAP3 (2015), "Draft 2015 Virginia P3 Project Pipeline", www.p3virginia.org/wp-content/uploads/2015/10/Clean-copy-Revisions-to-2015-PipelineOctober2620151.pdf.

Virginia addressed this regulatory coherence problem, in part, by adapting its PPP enabling statutes to produce a flexible and inclusive PPP programme (Gifford and Transue, 2015). From the outset, each of its PPP enabling acts instituted a state-wide, programmatic approach without geographic or political restrictions (HCA, QTFA, PPTA as amended, PPEA as amended). As the state's statutory framework developed, this programme flexibility extended to a nearly unlimited range of qualifying proposal types (solicited and unsolicited), facility types (transportation, education, utility, government), partner types, delivery approaches, and financing options (PPTA, as amended in 2001, 2005, and 2006; PPEA, as amended in 2003, 2005, 2007, 2008, and 2009). As a result, private parties encounter few limitations in these respects.

Virginia PPP projects have also faced limited legislative intervention. State law does not require legislative approval prior to facility procurement, relying instead on responsible public entities for project review, approvals, and management. Some argue that legislative approval at or near commercial close can preserve public accountability and protect the public interest. Limiting legislative involvement at such a late stage can greatly reduce the political risk that can discourage private participation (Rall, Reed, and Farber, 2010: 16, 18–19; Buxbaum and Ortiz: 2009, 13–14). To address public oversight concerns without introducing direct legislative approval, a 2015 PPTA amendment established the Transportation Public-Private Partnership Advisory Committee, which is comprised of members from the gubernatorially-appointed Commonwealth Transportation Board, legislative staff, and the executive branch, and charged with assessing whether proposed projects serve the public interest.

In addition to its inclusive statutes, Virginia's PPP programmes have developed implementation guidelines to help potential and active partners understand and navigate the state's PPP procurement procedures. In response to 2005 amendments to PPTA and PPEA requiring these guidelines, the state developed formal PPTA implementation guidelines in 2005, with updates in 2008, 2010, 2012, and 2014 (additional updates are under development) (Commonwealth of Virginia, 2005; 2008a; 2010; 2012; 2014; 2016). It developed equivalent PPEA implementation guidelines in 2002 with updates in 2006 and 2008 (additional updates are under development) (Commonwealth of Virginia, 2002; 2006a; 2006b; 2008b; 2015). These detailed guideline documents provide thorough descriptions of the PPP programme's objectives and organisational structure, as well as their project identification, screening, development, and procurement processes. Together these guidelines provide transparency and consistency for private-sector entities interested in providing investment and innovations to address the state's infrastructure needs.

Virginia's PPP programme also benefitted greatly from the formation of Virginia's Office of Public-Private Partnerships (VAP3), formerly the Office of Transportation Public-Private Partnerships (OTP3), following an independent PPTA programme review, to develop and implement the state's PPP programme and streamline long project development and implementation processes (Daito et al., 2013: 40; KPMG Infrastructure Advisory, 2010). The office works with seven transportation-related departments to develop PPP infrastructure projects and provides education and feedback by developing and disseminating implementation manuals and guidelines, presentations, forms, outreach events, and other resources to support relationships with the private sector and the general public (VAP3, 2015c; 2015a). (See the Administrative Capacity section below for additional discussion.)

Finally, Virginia's PPP programme works to develop public-interest projects that remain sufficiently attractive for private investment, even when public policy diverges from private-sector interests. For example, state policy encourages carpooling, typically exempting high occupancy vehicles (HOV) from tolls to the disadvantage of toll-collecting concessionaires. To accommodate both HOV policy and private financial viability, several Virginian PPP concession agreements include provisions ensuring lost-revenue compensation for concessionaires if/when HOV traffic exceeds a pre-determined rate. According to the I-95 Express Lanes agreement, for example, the state will pay 70% of the average toll for HOV vehicles exceeding 35-38% of total traffic flow (VDOT, 2012b: 13–14). For the first two quarters of operation in 2015, HOV traffic accounted for 32% of all traffic in these lanes, approaching the compensation threshold (Shenk, 2015a; 2015b). The 495 Express Lanes agreement includes a similar provision for HOV vehicles exceeding 24% of total traffic flow (VDOT, 2007). Such provisions offer a mechanism to accommodate both public and private sector interests to produce a mutually beneficial project.

Financial risks

Since PPPs offer access to private-sector capital investment and financing, they can present appealing options for public-sector decision makers looking to locate new or timely financing options for public infrastructure investment. Virginia does not currently use availability payments and has instead relied exclusively on revenue risk financing complemented by direct government funding.[3] For instance, private investments, supported by private activity bonds and federal TIFIA loans, enabled Virginia's 495 Express Lanes project just as the 2008 credit crisis undermined more traditional financing instruments (Daito et al., 2013: 43). Along with their many valuable and timely opportunities however, PPP approaches generate substantial and long-term design, revenue, and debt-related risks. Consequently, decision makers must carefully evaluate whether a PPP project's projected benefits outweigh its resultant risks and liabilities (Koelemay, 2015). Only projects fitting this criterion and addressing the public's long-term public interests should be considered for PPP procurement.

Appropriate project selection has formed an important component of Virginia's PPP program. Each of the enabling acts conditioned project approvals on formal findings of public need and/or public interest, particularly with respect to existing public sector transportation plans. In addition, while PPTA and PPEA exempt PPP projects from the Virginia Public Procurement Act, they require that responsible public entities develop equivalent procedures preserving competitiveness, protecting the public interest, and demonstrating that accepted projects provide sufficient benefits under PPP procurement when compared to their risks and to traditional procurement.

While Virginia has developed and/or completed many PPP projects, it has also rejected a large number (see Table 4.2). For some, like Route 460 and Odd Fellows Road, the state's screening evaluations determined that PPP procurement would not offer better value than more traditional procurement approaches (VAP3, 2015e; 2015b). Other proposals, like the NOVA Commuter Fast Ferry Service and the Powhite Parkway Extension, demonstrated insufficient economic viability or cost effectiveness (VAP3, 2014a; 2014b). These cases signal caution by responsible public entities using alternative procurement approaches only where they promise to meet the public's needs efficiently and effectively.

Even the best projects face real risks however, especially regarding debt repayment and investment returns under concession agreements lasting fifty years or more. Large and complex infrastructure projects depend on demand and revenue forecasts in advance of construction because capital investments in infrastructure assets typically become indivisible and immobile, exposing investors to revenue risk (Medda, 2007). Unfortunately, many projects fail to meet their demand forecasts. Up to 90% of transit projects worldwide have failed to meet their demand forecasts (Siemiatycki and Friedman, 2012), for example, and 20% to 30% differences between projections and actual demand are typical across the transportation sectors (Trujillo, Quinet, and Estache, 2002). Demand overestimation for toll roads has even exceeded observed traffic flows by up to 60% in some international cases (Checherita and Gifford, 2007). Despite careful project selection, several Virginia projects have experienced this predicament.

For example, the first toll road built under HCA, the Dulles Greenway connecting Leesburg with the Washington Dulles International Airport, failed to meet traffic projections after it opened in 1995 just as a real estate market downturn began. With revenues reaching only about one third of expectations, the project required debt restructuring and design and contract modifications between 1997 and 2013 to remain operational. A few years later, the Route 895 (Pocahontas Parkway) toll facility connecting Chesterfield and Henrico counties south of Richmond faced similar difficulties. With disappointing demand and earnings equalling less than half of expectations upon opening in 2002 – again attributable in part to a real estate downturn – the project experienced several contract modifications and owner changes with significant investment losses (Gifford, Bolaños, and Daito, 2014). The state was not responsible for paying the debt obligations in either case, nor did it provide bailouts. Instead, it relied on restructuring and contract modification processes to keep the facilities open, including allowing toll increases and a concession extension for the Dulles Greenway project. This approach reflects the US bankruptcy system's preference for debt restructuring over asset liquidation, a potential divergence from Europe's experience (Gifford, Bolaños, and Kweun, 2015a). Nevertheless, such experiences motivated statutory changes strengthening Virginia's proposal review processes and may have a chilling effect on PPP enthusiasm within investment markets and the public sector.

While Virginia's PPP project approvals have always depended on the reasonableness of their proposed designs, schedules, and financing plans, as the programme matured into the 21st century, the state legislature began strengthening PPTA and PPEA's review requirements, particularly with regard to risk. In 2007, for instance, an amendment to PPEA required additional review for proposed comprehensive agreements creating state tax-supported debt, requiring significant appropriations, or significantly altering state discretion over future service levels or service funding. A year later, a 2008 PPTA amendment required independent audits of all traffic, cost, and taxpayer liability estimates for projects whose estimated construction costs exceed USD 50 million. More recently, a 2015 amendment to PPTA required formal findings of public interest from responsible public entity chief executives, with concurrence from the Transportation Public-Private Partnerships Advisory Committee, prior to PPP procurement, providing detailed risk disclosures, outlining measures to address these risks, and demonstrating that project benefits outweigh the prevailing risks. Together, these statutory amendments have greatly strengthened the PPP programme's risk review procedures but have also raised concerns that project cancellation risks might discourage potential bidders from developing proposals.

Virginia's PPP programme has also encountered problems regarding user fees. While tolls and other user fees often form the foundation for PPP facilities' financial viability, pricing and implementation choices require careful consideration, especially in places where user fees have proven unpopular for customers. Virginia's PPP enabling statutes maintain public-sector regulatory authority over tolls and user-fee setting procedures, aiming to ensure viable private rates-of-return while also protecting users and encouraging facility use (Buxbaum and Ortiz 2009, 29–30, 40). While HCA originally gave the State Corporation Commission authority over tolling, PPTA and PPEA shifted user fee setting and approvals to the comprehensive agreements negotiated by responsible public entities. In practice, however, tolls can be difficult to implement due to technical challenges (e.g. electronic toll collection, congestion management pricing) and public resistance.

For example, under the Elizabeth River Crossing DBFOM project currently under construction, a large portion of the project's estimated USD 2.1 billion construction cost was to be financed through toll revenues, particularly USD 268 million in tolls collected from the existing tunnels starting several years before the project's completion (FHWA, 2014a). The public objected to the tolling plan, however (Reinhardt, 2012; Samuel, 2012a), and the project has since experienced several public-sector-initiated contract renegotiations to modify and delay tolling implementation (Samuel 2012b; Virginia Office of the Governor, 2014; VDOT, 2015). A Portsmouth resident even sued, arguing that VDOT imposed the tolls unlawfully, but a 2013 Virginia Supreme Court ruling decided the case in the state's favour (Elizabeth River Crossings OPCO, LLC v. Meeks, 749 S.E.2d 176 (Va. 2013); Gifford, Bolaños, and Daito, 2014). Despite this court decision, anti-tolling sentiment has solidified politically in Virginia and might discourage, or at least complicate, future PPP procurements using this important revenue source.

Cross-jurisdictional co-ordination

Qualifying PPP projects often entail wide scope to benefit from economies of scale and positive spillovers across jurisdictions. Virginia's recent I-95 Express Lanes and Elizabeth River Crossings projects, costing USD 925 million and USD 2.1 billion, respectively, with concession agreements lasting fifty years or more, demonstrate just how extensive PPPs can be (VAP3, 2015f; FHWA, 2014a; 2014b). These billion-plus dollar projects involve long-term co-ordination, co-operation, and management across dozens of actors and subnational governments (Koelemay, 2015), with affected jurisdictions often representing different views, risks, benefits, and responsibilities. A diversity of stakeholders can complicate co-ordination efforts and, given the United States' highly decentralised system of local governments, might discourage PPP use as a result (Mizell and Allain-Dupré, 2013: 18-19). In the Elizabeth River Crossings case, for example, leaders of the city of Portsmouth, were particularly concerned that its residents would be disproportionately affected by the imposition of tolls on river crossings that had previously been toll free.

The Virginia state government's exceptional (by US standards) control over its roadways may have simplified its PPP experience somewhat in the surface transportation sector. Unlike many states, only two of Virginia's 100 counties maintain their own roads; the state government assumed this responsibility during the Great Depression. As a result, VDOT supports 57 867 miles of state-maintained highways, 10 561 miles of urban streets, 12 600 bridges, 6 tunnels, 2 toll facilities, 4 ferry services, rest areas, and several commuter parking lots (VDOT, 2014; Gifford et al., 2015b). While this centralised control can simplify planning, it adds a substantial administrative burden for VDOT and limits county and local-government participation (Gifford, 2011).

Virginia's PPP statutes also require that proposal reviews consider a proposed project's compatibility with existing public infrastructure development plans and their objectives. PPP approval processes also provide sixty-day comment periods for affected jurisdictions. Responsible public entities must consider these comments before approving alternative procurement (QTFA; PPTA as amended in 2005; PPEA). The VAP3 also plays a role in co-ordination, information dissemination, and technical assistance.

Nonetheless, such activities cannot prevent all conflict. Existing transportation service providers may resist entry by new competition. Communities often oppose projects that increase traffic through their borders. In the I-95 Express Lanes case, original project plans included a 6-mile stretch through Arlington County and Alexandria connecting the District of Columbia and northern Virginia. Arlington County objected, ultimately suing in August 2009 to challenge the project's environmental reviews, potential for increased traffic congestion and emissions, and possible effects on minority populations. Facing mounting delays the state eventually revised the project to remove that portion (Goodman, 2011; Halsey, 2009), although an I-395 Express Lanes Extension came back under consideration in late 2015 (VDOT, 2016).

Administrative capacity

Most subnational governments shifting from traditional design-bid-build procurement approaches to an innovative PPP programme require new technical and administrative skills. PPPs introduce a range of new relationships, development processes, risk evaluations, and contract management requirements that challenge existing public and private-sector strategic, executive, institutional, and cross-cultural capacities. Adopting PPP procurement challenged the routines of Virginia's public sector, forcing agencies like VDOT to change focus and develop new relationships, organisational structures, skills, and management styles. In some cases, this meant shifting focus from physical infrastructure delivery to service provision. In many other cases, agencies developed new relationships with the private sector and with other public agencies to execute complex alternative financing and procurement approaches. In the process, many state agencies recognised the need for stronger public engagement as well, developing improved outreach, feedback, and information dissemination capacities. All these development, evaluation, management, and monitoring approaches required challenging institutional changes given the agencies' prevailing objectives, procedures, cultures, and contested political environments. Strong leadership, improved communication, and structural changes helped advance the transition (Gifford et al., 2015b).

The strongest administrative changes came with the formation of a dedicated PPP programme office. A PPTA programme assessment completed in 2010 found that the programme, as originally administered by various transportation sub-departments: 1) suffered from fragmented priorities, authority, and accountability; 2) lacked a multi-modal focus; 3) lacked a programmatic approach to its methods, processes, priorities, and funding; and ultimately, 4) demonstrated overly-long project development and implementation. To address these limitations, the report recommended the formation of a separate, multi-modal PPTA programme office that centralised PPP programme ownership, accountability, funding, and responsibility with the focus, funding, expertise, and standardised procedures necessary to support a robust and effective programme (KPMG Infrastructure Advisory, 2010). The resulting Virginia Office of Public-Private Partnerships office (VAP3, originally called the Office of Transportation Public-Private Partnerships, OTP3), was established in 2011. It greatly refocused the state's PPP program, developed a PPP-sensitive organisational culture with PPP-appropriate procedures, and improved public engagement and stakeholder outreach (VAP3, 2014c). Other subnational governments considering new or adapted PPP programmes often solicit guidance from VAP3 staff members. For example, the National Governors Association included the leader of the VAP3 in a fall 2015 showcase on PPPs in the capital of Arkansas. Soon after the current director's appointment in early 2014, a blog post from the widely read *Public Works Financing* characterised the office as "… the most powerful P3 incubator in the country…" (Reinhardt, n.d.).

Accountability and transparency

Since PPP procurement arrangements necessarily transfer infrastructure delivery responsibilities (and often their revenue streams) to private-sector actors, transparency, accountability and competitive procurement procedures are essential for protecting the public interest. Virginia's PPP enabling statutes and their subsequent amendments have endeavoured to provide this protection. First, while PPTA and PPEA (as amended) exempted qualifying facilities from the Virginia Public Procurement Act, they stipulated that responsible public entities develop equivalent procedures consistent with competitive negotiation and competitive sealed bidding. In addition, both acts required that responsible public entities justify the proposed alternative procurement based on "(i) the probable scope, complexity, or urgency of a project or (ii) risk sharing, added value, an increase in funding, or economic benefit from the project that would not otherwise be available."

Second, since Virginia relies on responsible public entities rather than legislative approval to review, approve, and manage its PPP projects, comprehensive and timely public information disclosures become essential (Rall, Reed, and Farber, 2010: 10, 12; Buxbaum and Ortiz, 2009: 24–27).Virginia's PPP statutes always required financial disclosures from private partners, but several amendments strengthened PPTA's and PPEA's disclosure requirements during the mid-2000s. For example, 2006 and 2007 amendments to both acts require public disclosure of all proposals within ten days of receipt. Interim and comprehensive agreements are made available for thirty-day public comment periods before finalisation, and procurement records for finalised comprehensive agreements are available to the public upon request.

Third, Virginia has strengthened its public PPP review provisions in recent years. In 2007, for example, the state legislature established the Public-Private Partnership Advisory Commission to review PPEA proposals valued between USD 3 million and USD 50 million and to promptly provide recommendations regarding proposed projects' state tax-supported debt, financial impacts, policy concerns, and business terms. Additional disclosure and review by appropriating bodies were also required for agreements involving tax-supported debt, unusual appropriations, or changes in state control. As noted previously, a similar 2015 amendment to PPTA established the Transportation Public-Private Partnership Advisory Committee with representatives from the Commonwealth Transportation Board, the executive branch, and legislative staff to determine whether proposed projects serve the public interest.

Following the proposal review and procurement phases, responsible public entities remain accountable for oversight. At the project level, PPP contractual agreements, including project-specific performance standards, can offer an additional tool for protecting the public interest and producing high-quality PPP facilities ahead of schedule and under budget. Virginia's flexible statutory framework allows for innovative project management and performance measurement systems as negotiated in comprehensive agreements. However, these approaches present challenges in practice. By shifting to new core activities, procurement methods, and relationships to manage innovative, uncertain, and complex PPP delivery mechanisms, public agencies often struggle without clear-cut, measureable results. This is particularly true as outside factors (e.g. public preferences, macroeconomic shifts, political shifts) drive project outcomes (Koelemay, 2015). As a result, while performance measurement offers management benefits, agencies accustomed to traditional procurement can find them difficult to implement for complex PPP projects (Gifford et al., 2015b).

Discussion

Given the US infrastructure market's decentralised governance and ongoing funding limitations, PPP approaches have become increasingly popular as subnational governments search for improved design, procurement, and funding solutions. While the federal government offers several support programmes and thirty-three states allow PPP approaches for transportation infrastructure delivery, challenges remain. With its multi-decade history, Virginia's PPP programme experience offers insights for other subnational governments. Three broad success factors emerge from the preceding case analysis, suggesting three recommendations for subnational governments developing PPPs.

First, Virginia's experience highlights the importance of developing a flexible and inclusive statutory framework that supports private-sector participation, accountability, and transparency without inviting political interference. Virginia's flexible and inclusive statutory framework, without legislative approval, opens attractive opportunities for public and private partners to formulate best-practice infrastructure delivery to meet the state's needs. While many states impose restrictions on their PPP programmes, Virginia's PPP enabling acts support a state-wide, programmatic approach without restrictions on qualifying proposal types (solicited vs. unsolicited), facility types, partner types, delivery approaches, or financing options. As a result, Virginia's programme presents few barriers to entry for private parties in these respects. In addition, the state's reliance on responsible public entities – rather than the legislature – to review, approve, and manage projects has limited political interference that might otherwise discourage private-sector participation.

Virginia has also developed a range of policies and procedures to preserve accountability and protect the public interest. For example, while PPTA and PPEA exempt qualifying facilities from the Virginia Public Procurement Act, they stipulate that responsible public entities must justify their PPP procurements and develop equivalent procedures consistent with competitive negotiation and competitive sealed bidding. Virginia's PPP statutes also include a range of provisions requiring timely public disclosure and comment periods, independent audits, and review by either the Public-Private Partnership Advisory Commission (PPEA) or the Transportation Public-Private Partnership Advisory Committee (PPTA) to determine whether proposed projects serve the public interest.

Second, not all infrastructure projects represent strong candidates for PPP procurement. Virginia's experience underscores the need to develop a rigorous selection and review process for projects. Under Virginia's careful project selection and review processes, candidate projects must address public needs and PPP proposals must demonstrate superior predicted outcomes compared to traditional public procurement alternatives. As a result, Virginia has developed and completed many PPP projects, but it has also rejected many. The state's willingness to say "no" to inappropriate projects, debt guarantees, and bailouts has done much to limit its financial risks. Nevertheless, given the wide-ranging risks facing PPPs, the state continues to strengthen its PPP review requirements, recently adding provisions for debt review, independent audits, and official findings of public interest.

Finally, Virginia's experience points to the value of developing a dedicated PPP programme office to centralise programme priorities, authority, funding, and processes, and to develop the internal expertise and external advisors needed to review and assess projects. Prior to VAP3's formation, the state's PPP programme lacked cohesive priorities, authority, accountability, and programmatic approaches to its methods, processes, and funding. VAP3's formation as a separate, multi-modal office centralised PPP programme ownership, accountability, funding, and responsibility, and provided the focus, expertise, and standardised procedures necessary to support a robust and effective program. The resulting office greatly refocused the state's PPP programme and developed a vital PPP-sensitive organisational culture with PPP-appropriate procedures. The office also maintains a set of legal, financial and technical capabilities through on-call staff augmentation contracts that provide specialised expertise needed for particular projects.

Table 4.3. Successes and challenges in the Virginia PPP case

Type of challenge	Factors facilitating success	Remaining challenges
Intergovernmental regulatory coherence	Flexible, inclusive statutory framework Limited political interference Virginia Office of Public-Private Partnerships	State and federal environmental regulations (e.g. I-495 Express Lanes) Statutory variation between US states (potential private-sector barrier)
Financial risks	Careful project selection, evaluation, and review	Demand and revenue risk evaluation (e.g. Dulles Greenway, Route 895) User-fee opposition (e.g. Elizabeth River Crossings)
Cross-jurisdictional co-ordination	Consideration of public infrastructure development plans and comments from affected jurisdictions	Stakeholder outreach and engagement (e.g. I-95 Express Lanes)
Administrative capacity	Virginia Office of Public-Private Partnerships	Transitioning bureaucratic tasks, processes, and procedures Stakeholder outreach and engagement
Accountability and transparency	Public-interest requirements Review bodies Public disclosure requirements	Project management, performance measurement, and oversight

Source: Authors' elaboration.

Despite these success factors, Virginia's PPPs still face important challenges (Table 4.3). Environmental regulations complicate already complex projects (e.g. I-495 Express Lanes) and financial risks often prove difficult to predict (e.g. Dulles Greenway, Route 895). In addition, growing public opposition to user fees threatens to discourage future PPP procurements using this revenue source (e.g. Elizabeth River Crossings). Administratively, new infrastructure delivery approaches like PPPs have required difficult transitions to new development, evaluation, management, and monitoring approaches that often clash with prevailing objectives, procedures, and cultures. Public outreach and stakeholder engagement has remained particularly challenging (e.g. Elizabeth River Crossings). Finally, while the state has greatly improved its PPP review and disclosure requirements, robust performance measurement, management, and oversight prove difficult to formulate and implement.

Conclusion

Ultimately, Virginia's ability to develop and adapt its PPP programme over its long history has proved essential to its continued relevance and viability. As the state continues to grapple with different challenges, its statutory flexibility, dedicated PPP office, and continued institutional learning will help its PPP programme evolve to meet the state's developing needs. Alongside FHWA's office of Innovative Programme Delivery, the Build America Transportation Investment Center, and organisations like the National Conference of State Legislatures' (NCSL), the American Association of State Highway and Transportation Officials' (AASHTO), and the National Governors Association (NGA), Virginia's PPP programme offers an ever evolving model to inform other subnational governments pursuing PPP opportunities.

Notes

1. This Virginia case analysis benefitted greatly from research conducted for the article, Gifford, J.L., and M. Transue (2015), "The Evolution of Virginia's Public-Private Partnership Enabling Statutes", *Journal of Corporation Law*. 41: 265-281.
2. Nominal dollars, unless otherwise noted.
3. The most recent draft "pipeline" documents from the Virginia Office of Public-Private Partnerships includes a conceptual project involving exploring the viability of using availability payments as a funding option (Virginia Office of Public-Private Partnerships, 2015f).

References

American Association of State Highway and Transportation Officials (2015), "Transportation Finance Clearinghouse".

American Society of Civil Engineers (2017), "2017 Infrastructure Report Card: A Comprehensive Assessment of America's Infrastructure", www.infrastructurereportcard.org (accessed 4 May 2015).

Buxbaum, J.N., and I.N. Ortiz (2009), "Public Sector Decision Making for Public-Private Partnerships: A Synthesis of Highway Practice", NCHRP Synthesis 391, National Cooperative Highway Research Program, Transportation Research Board, www.trb.org/Publications/Blurbs/156870.aspx.

Checherita, C., and J.L. Gifford (2007), "Risk Sharing in Public-Private Partnerships; General Considerations and an Evaluation of the US Practice in Road Transportation", in *Transportation Research Forum*, https://ageconsearch.umn.edu/bitstream/207820/2/2007_1B_PartFin_paper.pdf.

Commonwealth of Virginia (2016), "Implementation Manual and Guidelines for the Public-Private Transportation Act of 1995 (As Amended)", www.p3virginia.org/wp-content/uploads/2016/01/PPTA-Implementation-Manual-01-04-2016-final-posted-to-website-before-Jan-CTB.pdf (accessed 29 October 2015).

Commonwealth of Virginia (2015), "Implementation Manual and Guidelines for the Public-Private Education Facilities and Infrastructure Act of 2002", www.p3virginia.org/wp-content/uploads/2015/06/PPEA-Draft-06_25_15-.pdf (accessed 29 October 2017).

Commonwealth of Virginia (2014), "Implementation Manual and Guidelines for the Public-Private Transportation Act of 1995 (As Amended)", www.virginiadot.org/office_of_transportation_public-private_partnerships/resources/UPDATED_PPTA_Implementation_Manual_11-07-14_FOR_POSTING_TO_WEBSITE_-_changes_accepted.pdf (accessed 29 October 2015).

Commonwealth of Virginia (2012), "Public-Private Transportation Act of 1995, (as Amended): Implementation Manual and Guidelines", www.p3virginia.org/wp-content/uploads/2015/03/PPTA-Implementation-Manual_May_21_2012.pdf (accessed 29 October 2015).

Commonwealth of Virginia (2010), "Public-Private Transportation Act of 1995, (as Amended): Implementation Manual and Guidelines", www.p3virginia.org/wp-content/uploads/2015/03/PPTA-Implementation-Manual_FINAL_December_08_2010.pdf (accessed 29 October 2015).

Commonwealth of Virginia (2008a), "Public-Private Transportation Act of 1995 (as Amended): Implementation Guidelines", www.p3virginia.org/wp-content/uploads/2015/03/PPTA-Final-Guideline-Change-December-2008-Final.pdf (accessed 20 November 2015).

Commonwealth of Virginia (2008b), "Public-Private Education Facilities and Infrastructure Act of 2002 as Amended: Guidelines and Procedures", https://dgs.virginia.gov/globalassets/business-units/deb/documents/ppea-adminstration-guidelines-2008.pdf.

Commonwealth of Virginia (2006a), "Public-Private Education Facilities and Infrastructure Act of 2002: Procedures", https://dgs.virginia.gov/globalassets/business-units/deb/documents/ppea_may-2006.pdf.

Commonwealth of Virginia (2006b), "Public-Private Education Facilities and Infrastructure Act of 2002 as Amended: Procedures".

Commonwealth of Virginia (2005), "Public-Private Transportation Act of 1995 (as Amended): Implementation Guidelines", www.p3virginia.org/wp-content/uploads/2015/03/PPTA_Guidelines_FINAL_Revised_081205.pdf (accessed 11 November 2015).

Commonwealth of Virginia (2002), "Public-Private Education Facilities and Infrastructure Act of 2002: Procedures", https://law.lis.virginia.gov/vacodepopularnames/the-public-private-education-facilities-and-infrastructure-act-of-2002/.

Custos, D., and J. Reitz (2010), "Public-Private Partnerships", *American Journal of Comparative Law* 58: 555–84.

Daito, N., Z. Chen, J.L. Gifford, T. Porter, and J.E. Gudgel (2013), "Implementing Public Private Partnerships during Challenging Economic Times: Case Study of the 495 Express Lanes on the Virginia Portion of the Washington Capital Beltway Project (USA)", *Case Studies on Transport Policy* 1: 35–45.

Elizabeth River Crossings OPCO, LLC v. Meeks, 749 S.E.2d 176 (Va. 2013).

Esty, B.C. (2003), *Modern Project Finance: A Casebook*, Wiley.

FHWA (Federal Highway Administration) (2015), "Private Activity Bonds (PABS)", webpage, www.fhwa.dot.gov/ipd/finance/tools_programs/federal_debt_financing/private_activity_bonds/ (accessed 25 March 2018).

FHWA (2014a), "Project Profiles: Downtown Tunnel / Midtown Tunnel / MLK Extension".

FHWA (2014b), "Project Profiles: I-95 HOV/HOT Lanes", www.fhwa.dot.gov/ipd/project_profiles/va_i95.aspx (accessed 25 March 2018).

FHWA (2014c), "Highway Statistics 2013: Revenues Used by Local Government for Highways -- 2012", October, www.fhwa.dot.gov/policyinformation/statistics/2013/lgf1.cfm (accessed 20 November 2015).

FHWA (2014d), "Financing Federal-Aid Highways", archived webpage, www.fhwa.dot.gov/policy/olsp/financingfederalaid/fund.cfm (accessed 25 March 2018).

FHWA (2014e) "Highway Statistics 2013: Revenues Used By States for Highways - 2013", December. www.fhwa.dot.gov/policyinformation/statistics/2013/sf1.cfm#foot1 (accessed 20 November 2015).

FHWA (2006), "Design-Build Effectiveness Study", US Department of Transportation. www.fhwa.dot.gov/reports/designbuild/designbuild.pdf (accessed 20 November 2015).

FHWA (n.d. a), "63-20 Nonprofit Public Benefit Corporation".

FHWA (n.d. b), "How the Center Does Business", www.fhwa.dot.gov/ipd/how_business/ (accessed 25 March 2018).

FHWA (n.d. c), "P3 Defined", www.fhwa.dot.gov/ipd/p3/defined (accessed 21 November 2015).

FHWA (n.d. d), "State P3 Legislation", www.fhwa.dot.gov/ipd/p3/legislation/(accessed November 21, 2015).

Geddes, R. Richard and Benjamin L. Wagner (2013), "Why Do US States Adopt Public–private Partnership Enabling Legislation?" *Journal of Urban Economics* 78 (November), pp. 30–41.

Gifford, J.L. (2011), "Policy Options for Secondary Road Construction and Management in the Commonwealth of Virginia", *SSRN Scholarly Paper*, ID 1865957, Social Science Research Network, Rochester, NY, http://papers.ssrn.com/abstract=1865957 (accessed 20 November 2015).

Gifford, J.L. (2010), "State Infrastructure Banks: A Virginia Perspective", *SSRN Scholarly Paper*, ID 1714466, Social Science Research Network, Rochester, NY, http://papers.ssrn.com/abstract=1714466 (accessed 20 November 2015).

Gifford, J.L. (2003), *Flexible Urban Transportation*, Elsevier.

Gifford, J.L., L. Bolaños and N. Daito (2014), "Renegotiation of Transportation Public-Private Partnerships: The US Experience", *International Transport Forum Discussion Papers*, OECD Publishing, Paris, www.oecd-ilibrary.org/content/workingpaper/5jrw2xz9xhs1-en.

Gifford, J.L., L. Bolaños, and J.Y. Kweun (2015a), "Bankruptcy Policy and Surface Transportation Public-Private Partnerships: A Comparative Analysis of the US and Europe", 4th International Joint Conference in the Public-Private Partnership Conference Series.

Gifford, J.L., L. Bolaños, M. Transue, and J.Y. Kweun (2015b), "The Governance of Surface Transportation in the 21st Century: VDOT Institutional Responses to Environmental Changes", 19th Annual Conference of the International Society for New Institutional Economics.

Gifford, J.L., and M. Transue (2015). "The Evolution of Virginia's Public-Private Partnership Enabling Statutes", *Journal of Corporation Law*, 41, pp. 265-281.

Goodman, Christy (2011), "New HOT Lane Plan for Virginia's I-95 Corridor", *The Washington Post*, February 4, sec. Metro, www.washingtonpost.com/wp-dyn/content/article/2011/02/03/AR2011020305923.html.

Halsey, A. III. (2009), "Lawsuit Over Virginia HOT Lanes Spurs Mixed Reactions from Advocacy Groups", *The Washington Post*, August 21, sec. Metro, www.washingtonpost.com/wp-dyn/content/article/2009/08/20/AR2009082003348.html (accessed 21 November 2015).

Halsey, A. III, and J. Eilperin (2014), "House Passes Stop-Gap Bill to Fund Transportation through May", *The Washington Post*, 15 July, www.washingtonpost.com/local/trafficandcommuting/house-passes-stop-gap-bill-to-fund-transportation/2014/07/15/fe65537c-0c2f-11e4-b8e5-d0de80767fc2_story.html (accessed 21 November 2015).

Hecht, J. (2015), "Are Availability Payment Obligations Debt?" *Public Works Financing*, September.

History.com (2015), "Virginia - US States", www.history.com/topics/us-states/virginia (accessed 21 November 2015).

Istrate, E., and R. Puentes (2011), "Moving Forward on Public-Private Partnerships: US and International Experience with PPP Units", Brookings-Rockefeller Project on State and Metropolitan Innovation, www.brookings.edu/research/moving-forward-on-public-private-partnerships-u-s-and-international-experience-with-ppp-units/.

Koelemay, D. (2015), "To P3 or Not to P3, That Is the Question", Virginia Office of Public-Private Partnerships: Director's Blog, 9 September.

KPMG Infrastructure Advisory (2010), "Commonwealth of Virginia PPTA Program Assessment - Phase I Draft Diagnostic Report", 3 May, www.virginiadot.org/news/resources/statewide/ppta_assessment_report_final_052410.pdf (accessed 6 November 2015).

Levy, S.M. (1996), *Build, Operate, Transfer: Paving the Way for Tomorrow's Infrastructure.*, Wiley & Sons, New York.

Medda, Francesca (2007), "A Game Theory Approach for the Allocation of Risks in Transport Public Private Partnerships", *International Journal of Project Management* 25 (3), pp. 213–18, http://dx.doi.org/10.1016/j.ijproman.2006.06.003.

Mizell, L., and D. Allain-Dupré (2013), "Creating Conditions for Effective Public Investment: Sub-National Capacities in a Multi-Level Governance Context", *OECD Regional Development Working Papers*, No. 2013/04, OECD Publishing, Paris, http://dx.doi.org/10.1787/5k49j2cjv5mq-en.

Morris, D.Z. (2015), "Highway Funding Is Running out of Road -- Again", *Fortune*, 10 July, http://fortune.com/2015/07/10/highway-funding-running-out/.

National Governors Association Center for Best Practices (n.d.), "Transportation Funding and Financing", webpage, www.nga.org/cms/center/issues/eet/transportation-funding-financing (accessed 25 March 2018).

OECD (2017), "Subnational Governments in OECD Countries: Key Data", OECD, www.oecd.org/regional/regional-policy/Subnational-governments-in-OECD-Countries-Key-Data-2015.pdf (accessed 15 December 2015).

OECD (2014), "Recommendation of the Council on Effective Public Investment Across Levels of Government", 12 March 2014, www.oecd.org/regional/regional-policy/Principles-Public-Investment.pdf.

Puentes, R., and J. Thompson (2012), "Banking on Infrastructure: Enhancing State Revolving Funds for Transportation", Brookings-Rockefeller Project on State and Metropolitan Innovation, www.brookings.edu/~/media/research/files/papers/2012/9/12-state-infrastructure-investment-puentes/12-state-infrastructure-investment-puentes.pdf (accessed 13 November 2015).

Rall, J. (2014), "Public-Private Partnerships for Transportation: A Toolkit for Legislators -- February 2014 Updates and Corrections", National Conference of State Legislatures. www.ncsl.org/documents/transportation/NCSL-PPPTOOLKIT-update-Feb2014.pdf (accessed 20 November 2015).

Rall, J., J.B. Reed and N.J. Farber (2010), "Public-Private Partnerships for Transportation: A Toolkit for Legislators", National Conference of State Legislatures, www.ncsl.org/documents/transportation/PPPTOOLKIT.pdf (accessed 25 September 2015).

Reinhardt, W.G. (2012), "Midtown Financial Close Ignites Virginia Politics", *Public Works Financing*, April, www.pwfinance.net/document/research_reprints/1_Midtown_corrected.pdf (accessed December 8, 2014).

Reinhardt, W.G. (2011), "The Role of Private Investment in Meeting US Transportation Infrastructure Needs", The American Road and Transportation Builders Association Transportation Development Foundation (ARTBATDF), www.pwfinance.net/document/research_reports/0%20artba.pdf (accessed 12 November 2015).

Reinhardt, W.G. (n.d.), "Virginia's P3 Czar: Doug Koelemay", *Public Works Financing*, blog post, April, http://pwfinance.net/virginias-p3-czar-doug-koelemay/ (accessed 15 May 2017).

Rubin, R. (2015), "House Passes $8 Billion in Stopgap Funding for US Highways", *Bloomberg Politics*, 15 July, www.bloomberg.com/politics/articles/2015-07-15/house-passes-8-billion-in-stopgap-funding-for-u-s-highways (accessed 21 November 2015).

Samuel, P. (2013), "How Fluor-Lane Widened the 495 Capital Beltway from 8 to 12 Lanes INTERVIEW", *Toll Roads News*, 8 May.

Samuel, P. (2012a), "Toll Projects Generate Controversy in Virginia", *Toll Roads News*, 9 April.

Samuel, P. (2012b), "Virginia Gone to Financial Close on $2.1b Norfolk Crossings P3, Compromises on Toll Timing, Coverage", *Toll Roads News*, 20 April.

Seely, B.E. (1987), *Building the American Highway System: Engineers as Policy Makers*, Temple University Press, Philadelphia.

Shenk, S. (2015a), "I-95 Tolls Bring in $9 Million in First Quarter", *Fredericksburg.com*, 25 April, www.fredericksburg.com/news/transportation/i--tolls-bring-in-million-in-first-quarter/article_c198630e-fe30-5d82-be37-9fe4e0929232.html (accessed 21 November 2015).

Shenk, S. (2015b), "I-95 Express Lanes Continue to Rake in the Money, Ringing up $15 Million in the Second Quarter", *Fredericksburg.com*, 11 July, www.fredericksburg.com/news/transportation/i--express-lanes-continue-to-rake-in-the-money/article_4913b520-593e-533e-8bb4-f1198c2ae7f5.html (accessed 21 November 2015).

Siemiatycki, Matti, and Jonathan Friedman (2012), "The Trade-Offs of Transferring Demand Risk on Urban Transit Public–Private Partnerships", *Public Works Management & Policy* 17 (3), pp. 283–302, http://dx.doi.org/10.1177/1087724X12436993.

Trujillo, L., E. Quinet and A. Estache (2002), "Dealing with Demand Forecasting Games in Transport Privatization", *Transport Policy* 9 (4), pp. 325–34.

US Bureau of Economic Analysis (2014), "Regional Data, GDP & Personal Income", www.bea.gov/iTable/index_regional.cfm (accessed 21 November 2015).

US Census Bureau (2015a), "US and World Population Clock", www.census.gov/popclock/(accessed 15 December 2015).

US Census Bureau (2015b), "State & County Quick Facts – Virginia", 15 October, www.census.gov/quickfacts/VA.

US Congressional Budget Office (2015), "Public Spending on Transportation and Water Infrastructure, 1956-2014", www.cbo.gov/publication/49910 (accessed 15 December 2015).

USDOT (2015a), "National Transportation Statistics Table 1-1: System Mileage Within the United States (Statute Miles)", www.rita.dot.gov/bts/sites/rita.dot.gov.bts/files/publications/national_transportation_statistics/html/table_01_01.html (accessed 20 November 2015).

USDOT (2015b), "National Transportation Statistics Table 1-3: Number of US Airports", www.rita.dot.gov/bts/sites/rita.dot.gov.bts/files/publications/national_transportation_statistics/html/table_01_03.html (accessed 20 November 2015).

USDOT (2015c), "Beyond Traffic", www.transportation.gov/sites/dot.gov/files/docs/Draft_Beyond_Traffic_Framework.pdf (accessed 15 December 2015).

USDOT (2015d), "About BATIC", 29 September, www.transportation.gov/buildamerica/about (accessed 25 March 2018).

US General Accounting Office (1999), "Public-Private Partnerships: Terms Related to Building and Facility Partnerships", GAO/GGD-99-71, www.gao.gov/special.pubs/Gg99071.pdf (accessed 20 November 2015).

US General Accounting Office (1997), "Surface Transportation: States Are Experimenting With Design-Build Contracting", www.gao.gov/products/RCED-97-138R (accessed 20 November 2015).

US House of Representatives, Committee on Transportation and Infrastructure, Panel on Public-Private Partnerships (2014), "Public Private Partnerships: Balancing the Needs of the Public and Private Sectors to Finance the Nation's Infrastructure", Washington, DC, http://transportation.house.gov/uploadedfiles/p3_panel_report.pdf (accessed 15 December 2015).

US Securities and Exchange Commission (2012), "Investor Bulletin: Municipal Bonds", 15 June, www.sec.gov/investor/alerts/municipalbonds.htm (accessed 20 November 2015).

US Treasury Department (2011), "Treasury Analysis of Build America Bonds Issuance and Savings", www.treasury.gov/initiatives/recovery/Documents/BABs%20Report.pdf (accessed 21 November 2015).

VAP3 (2015a), "Manuals, Guidelines, Presentations, and Resources", www.p3virginia.org/ppta-resources/ (accessed 25 March 2018).

VAP3 (2015b), "Odd Fellows Road Interchange".

VAP3 (2015c), "Office Information", webpage, www.p3virginia.org/office-information/ (accessed 29 October 2015).

VAP3 (2015d), "Projects", webpage, www.p3virginia.org/p3-projects/ (accessed 29 October 2015).

VAP3 (2015e), "Route 460 Corridor".

VAP3 (2015f), "Draft 2015 Virginia P3 Project Pipeline", www.p3virginia.org/wp-content/uploads/2015/10/Clean-copy-Revisions-to-2015-PipelineOctober2620151.pdf (accessed 6 November 2015).

VAP3 (2014a), "Commuter Fast Ferry Service (NOVA)".

VAP3 (2014b), "Powhite Parkway Extension (Richmond)".

VAP3 (2014c), "Public Engagement", www.p3virginia.org/public-engagement/ (accessed 29 October 2015).

VAP3 (2013), "Public-Private Transportation Act Projects", www.p3virginia.org/wp-content/uploads/2014/12/2013_PPTA_Portfolio_Map_final1.pdf (accessed 25 September 2015).

VDOT (Virginia Department of Transportation), (2016), "I-395 Express Lanes Extension", www.virginiadot.org/projects/northernvirginia/395_express.asp (accessed 10 June 2016).

VDOT (2015), "Gov. McAuliffe Announces Deal Ensuring No Tolls on the MLK Freeway Extension in Portsmouth", Virginia Department of Transportation, 10 July, www.driveert.com/wp-content/uploads/2013/11/Governor-McAuliffe-Announces-Deal-Ensuring-No-Tolls-on-the-MLK-Freeway-Extension-in-Portsmouth.pdf.

VDOT (2014), "Virginia's Highway System", www.virginiadot.org/about/vdot_hgwy_sys.asp (accessed 16 November 2015).

VDOT (2012a), "American Recovery and Reinvestment Act", www.virginiadot.org/newsroom/stimulus_info.asp (accessed 15 December 2015).

VDOT (2012b), "Comprehensive Agreement Relating to the I-95 HOV/HOT Lanes Project".

VDOT (2007), "Amended and Restated Comprehensive Agreement Relating to the Route 495 HOT Lanes in Virginia Project".

VDOT (2006), "The History of Roads in Virginia", Virginia Department of Transportation, www.virginiadot.org/about/resources/historyofrds.pdf (accessed 21 November 2015).

Virginia General Assembly (1994), "Senate Joint Resolution 17".

Virginia General Assembly (1993), "Senate Joint Resolution 241".

Virginia General Assembly (1986), "State of the Commonwealth Address -- Governor Gerald L. Baliles", S. Doc. 2-B.

Virginia General Assembly (n.d.), "About the General Assembly", http://virginiageneralassembly.gov/virginiaLegislature.php?secid=20&activesec=2#!hb=1&mainContentTabs=4&content=4.includes/contentTemplate.php%3Ftid%3D52%26ctype%3Db%26cid%3D31 (accessed 21 November 2015).

Virginia General Assembly, Joint Subcommittee Studying Privatization of Certain State Government Functions (1995), "Final Report of the Joint Subcommittee Studying Privatization of Certain State Government Functions", S. Doc. 55.

Virginia Office of Intermodal Planning and Investment (2010), "Virginia Surface Transportation Plan 2035", www.vtrans.org/resources/VSTP_Entire_Report.pdf (accessed 16 November 2015).

Virginia Office of Intermodal Planning and Investment (2015), "VTrans2040: Vision -- Virginia's Statewide Multimodal Long-Range Transportation Policy Plan", Commonwealth Transportation Board, www.vtrans.org/resources/VTrans2040_Draft_Vision_Document_32415.pdf (accessed 16 November 2015).

Virginia Office of the Governor (2014), "Governor McAuliffe Announces Initial Toll Rates Will Be Cut in Half for the Downtown/Midtown Tunnels Project in Hampton Roads", Virginia Department of Transportation, 15 January, https://governor.virginia.gov/newsroom/newsarticle?articleId=2593.

ORGANISATION FOR ECONOMIC CO-OPERATION AND DEVELOPMENT

The OECD is a unique forum where governments work together to address the economic, social and environmental challenges of globalisation. The OECD is also at the forefront of efforts to understand and to help governments respond to new developments and concerns, such as corporate governance, the information economy and the challenges of an ageing population. The Organisation provides a setting where governments can compare policy experiences, seek answers to common problems, identify good practice and work to co-ordinate domestic and international policies.

The OECD member countries are: Australia, Austria, Belgium, Canada, Chile, the Czech Republic, Denmark, Estonia, Finland, France, Germany, Greece, Hungary, Iceland, Ireland, Israel, Italy, Japan, Korea, Latvia, Lithuania, Luxembourg, Mexico, the Netherlands, New Zealand, Norway, Poland, Portugal, the Slovak Republic, Slovenia, Spain, Sweden, Switzerland, Turkey, the United Kingdom and the United States. The European Union takes part in the work of the OECD.

OECD Publishing disseminates widely the results of the Organisation's statistics gathering and research on economic, social and environmental issues, as well as the conventions, guidelines and standards agreed by its members.

OECD PUBLISHING, 2, rue André-Pascal, 75775 PARIS CEDEX 16
(85 2018 17 1 P) ISBN 978-92-64-30485-7 – 2018

www.ingramcontent.com/pod-product-compliance
Lightning Source LLC
Chambersburg PA
CBHW061219240926
51846CB00006B/1286
9789264304857